MEDIA AND MARKET FORCES : CHALLENGES AND OPPORTUNITIES

About the Editors

V. S. Gupta, currently Professor at Haryana Agricultural University, was awarded the UNDP Fellowship for training in Europe and selected for the Journalist Fellowship Award for working in the area of Environment and Development. He conceptualised and implemented as Course Director the Post-Graduate Diploma in Agricultural Journalism and Refresher Course in Communication and Writing Skills in the university. He has written and edited over half a dozen books including *Media and Development, Third Revolution in Indian Perspective, National Media Policy*, and *Media Policy and Nation Building*, singly and jointly. He is the Country Representative for the Asian Media Information and Communication Centre (AMIC), Singapore. His forthcoming book is *Communication Technology, Media Policy and National Development—An Indian Perspective.*

Rajeshwar Dyal is currently working as Media Advisor with Friedrich-Ebert-Foundation, which aims at democratisation and pluralism in media, organising media activities with media in the government and private sector, academia from various departments and other research institutions. He was with the Indian Institute of Mass Communication, New Delhi for 15 years prior to joining the present assignment in 1992. He has an experience of more than 20 years in communication research and training and interaction with national and international media organisations and activities. With Prof. V. S. Gupta, he has edited *Rural Press—Problems and Prospects, and National Media Policy.*

MEDIA AND MARKET FORCES
Challenges and Opportunities

Proceedings of the Regional Seminars and the National Colloquium

Edited by

V. S. GUPTA
RAJESHWAR DYAL

Published for

AMIC
FRIEDRICH EBERT STIFTUNG

by

CONCEPT PUBLISHING COMPANY, NEW DELHI-110059

Proceedings of the Regional Seminars and the National Colloquium organised at various places by AMIC-India in collaboration with Friedrich Ebert Stiftung.

Regional Seminars

29-30 June 1996 at Hyderabad
27-28 July 1996 at Patna
10-11 August 1996 at Indore
15-16 September 1996 at Shimla
5 October 1996 at Bombay

National Colloquium

19-20 October, 1996 at New Delhi

ISBN 81-7022-698-8

First Published 1998

Published and Printed by

Ashok Kumar Mittal
Concept Publishing Company
A/15-16, Commercial Block,
Mohan Garden,
NEW DELHI - 110059 (India)
Phones: 5554042, 5504042
Fax: (011) 5598898

CONTENTS

ANNEXURES

FOREWORD

In 1993, The World Bank published two booklets : Poverty Reduction in South Asia and Ten Lessons from East Asia. The first dealt with the distressingly slow pace of poverty reduction in India and the other South Asian countries. The second focused on the East Asian miracle and the efforts of policymakers everywhere to search for lessons from East Asia's enormous success in economic development.

The East Asian economies are diverse-comprising some of the most populous and the least, some of the most resource rich and some of the poorest, of the world's countries. Yet, to quote the World Bank, in just 25 years "absolute poverty fell by two-thirds on average, population growth declined rapidly and health and education improved markedly". The success of development in East Asia is legendary.

India encompasses, within its borders, the diversity as well as the opportunities of East Asia. There is a miracle waiting to happen. A tiger waiting to be uncaged. This calls for investment in people, participatory development and institutional reform. There is need for clarity of vision and consistency of purpose and policy. The media have a crucial role to play as catalyst, chronical and social mobilizer.

As the world moves inexorably into the information age, the old distinctions are blurring and the media are becoming multimedia as converging communication technologies and the digital revolution necessitate change. The media not only influence market forces but are, in turn, influenced by them.

The media in India reflect the forces of change not only in production and distribution but also in their efforts to explore and exploit the opportunities in cyberspace.

AMIC has endeavoured to assist the region's media with

conferences, seminars and workshops focusing on changing technologies and economies and by trying to impart the new skills that the new times require. In India, the encouragement and support of the New Delhi Office of the Friedrich-Ebert-Stiftung (FES) have enabled AMIC-India to organize workshops and seminars designed to stimulate debate and discussion on media issues of national concern : media and development; rural press : problems and prospects; national media policy and, most recently, media and market forces. This is indeed a partnership for progress. It is our hope that this valuable support will continue in the years ahead to the benefit of communication practitioners, researchers and scholars and the media in the country.

VIJAY MENON
Secretary-General

INTRODUCTION

The exponential growth in the media industry and particularly in the electronic and satellite communication, witnessed during the recent years in India has changed the media scenario in the country as never before. The application of technology and intervention of market forces are the two dominant factors which have led to dramatic changes in the contemporary media situation. In the process of economic liberalisation that the country is witnessing over the last few years, the market forces are increasingly becoming a determining factor. Various other changes in the market place are also having a profound impact on the way the business of media is conducted. These include the changing psyche of the consumers and manufacturers in the industry, increasing dependence of computers in the workplace and technological development in the media.

Economic liberalisation has also meant increasing competition particularly in the area of television. The opening up of the economy has witnessed not only influx of foreign networks beaming into the Indian market, but many Indian companies have been able to uplink from various satellites operating from abroad. Today many publishing houses are diversifying into television production.

As India continues its march into 21st Century, many more changes are in the offing. In order to meet the demands of vastly expanding clientele, the publishing houses, FM radio, satellite television are in for changes in priorities and work culture. The new technologies have demolished the monopoly of state-run channels and rendered ineffective the regulatory mechanism framed in different era.

It was with this backdrop in view that AMIC India with support from Friedrich Ebert Stiftung (FES) decided to ogranise a series of five seminars during 1996—Hyderabad,

29-30 June; Patna, 27-28 July; Indore, 10-11 August; Shimla, 15-16 September and Bombay, 5 October 1996 and as a finale to the series of these seminars a National Colloquium was organised at the India International Centre, New Delhi on 19-20 October 1996. These seminars and the National Colloquium provided an opportunity to focus attention on the issues involved and take note of the developing scenario. The participants—media professionals and practitioners, members from the academic institutes, non-governmental organisations (NGOs) and voluntary bodies, scholars and social activists, brought their varied and rich experience to bear upon the discussion on some of the critical issues through presentations made by them. Some of these papers alongwith a number of Annexures have been put together in this publication for wider dissemination and to be of use for reference and consultation by the students and teachers of journalism, media practitioners and all other interested in the emerging media developments in the country. It has not been possible to take all the papers presented at these seminars; only some of the selected ones have been used in this publication for wider public discussion and debate.

During the course of the deliberations of these seminars we came across differing perceptions. In our Hyderabad seminar, deep concern was expressed at the newly emerging trends in the contemporary media and the debasement of Indian cultural traditions by market forces; at Patna, deep distress was voiced as to the failure of media in not warning the general public about the financial scams by the non-banking institutions in the State; in Indore, once again, the view was expressed that the media was catering more to the needs of handful of market forces and was unrelated to the realities of the society. The Seminar at Shimla came up with concrete suggestions that institutional checks for journalism profession should be evolved. The profession should be licenced on the pattern of medical and law profession and the licence would remain valid till such time as the journalists adhere to the professional ethics. The perception obtained at the Bombay seminar was quite different; that there was nothing wrong with the market forces dominating the media and that the happiness of an individual was in a large measure proportionate to his bank balance.

The National Colloquium, however, gave us different insight and perception. There was deep regret that public service broadcasting was not being given proper priority and that the electronic media was encouraging unhealthy social practices by promoting harmful consumer products. A number of speakers were of the opinion that in India, television at present appears to be following the path of networks elsewhere in the world where privatisation and commercialisation together act as major forces can be instrumental in influencing and shaping the very nature of medium. Sometimes it appears that because of the impact of market forces, and a consequence thereof, the media has contributed towards making India a consumers' paradise. In our race towards material acquisition we are throwing to winds our value based culture and heritage. The result of free wheeling market of media, if allowed unchecked, will affect all possible aspects of the social milieu—cultural, educational as well as political.

The Friedrich Ebert Stiftung Resident Representative, Mr. Horst Mund succinctly summed up the media scenario by saying : advertising revenues will grow and keep growing, only when viewership keeps growing, larger and larger. This is ensured by providing entertainment, more entertainment and more entertainment, 24 hours a day, 365 days a year. Undoubtedly, entertainment of the viewers is also important, but so much of importance and all kinds of entertainment.

The situation was sought to be rectified by several useful and practical proposals—public service broadcasting, community radio stations, alternative media, establishing more franchise radio and T.V. stations by the academic institutions and encouraging programmes in the areas of societal concern—environmental and consumer protection, empowerment of women, distant education and health.

We take this opportunity of expressing our deep gratitude to all the participants, observers, chairpersons and rapporteurs of various sessions and the authorities of the host institutions, who had collaborated in holding these seminars.

We would particularly like to place on record our deep gratitude to the veteran journalist, P. Venkateshwara and Prof. Abdur Rahim from Hyderabad; Mr. Uttam Sengupta, Resident Editor, *Times of India*, Patna edition; and the SRC-PCU team comprising Mr. Neeraj Labh and Ms. Sujata Sharma, Prof. A. A. Abbasi, Vice-Chancellor, Devi Ahilya University, Indore and Dr. P. N. Mishra, Chairman of *Utkarsha*, who coordinated the seminar at Indore; Mr. Kanwar Sandhu, Resident Editor, *Indian Express*, Chandigarh; Mr. Adarsh Sood, Mayor, Shimla Municipal Corporation; Mr. Vepa Rao, Chairman of the Department of Journalism, and the Seminar Coordinator, Dr. Vir Bala Aggarwal, also from the Department of Journalism; Himachal Pradesh University, Shimla; Mr. G. T. Balani, the AMIC India Representative from West Zone and the Coordinator of the Bombay Regional Seminar.

We also feel deeply obliged to Mr. Upendra Vajpeyi, General Secretary, National Media Centre; Mr. Ajit Bhattacharjea, Director, Press Institute of India; Mr. N. S. Jagannathan, Veteran Journalist; who guided our delebrations at the National Colloquium.

We received valuable guidance and support from AMIC Secretary General, Mr. Vijay Menon and the Resident Representative, FES, Mr. Horst Mund. We also acknowledge the valuable assistance extended by our other colleagues in AMIC India and the FES, New Delhi. We hope that the papers presented at these seminars and the National Colloquium which we have included in this book will go a long way in encouraging the debate and discussions on the impact of market forces on media in the country. We also hope that some of the suggestions will help to curb *junk journalism*, frothy entertainment leading to cultural alienation, and crass commercialisation.

And finally we place on record our gratitude to the Friedrich Ebert Stiftung for sponsoring these seminars and National Colloquium and also for the support in bringing this publication.

RAJESHWAR DYAL
Senior Advisor (Media) FES

V. S. GUPTA
Country Representative, AMIC

KEYNOTE ADDRESS

Let me, first of all, congratulate the Asian Media Information and Communication Centre (AMIC) for organising a nationwide debate on this subject with five regional seminars and a national colloquium at a very appropriate time when the media and communications scenario in India and other developing countries is changing at an accelerating speed, making the task of policy makers and media professionals a daunting one. The Friedrich-Ebert-Stiftung attaches great importance to the deliberations of this colloquium. We hope the discussions among communication experts will go a long way in facing the challenges of market forces and its relationship with the media.

In the present situation of economic liberalisation in India and other developing countries, market forces are playing a prominent role in the field of media and communications besides the economic and business fields. After the gulf war, satellite and cable television have grown at a tremendous speed all over Asia. In India besides the foreign satellite channels, large number of private channels in Hindi and several other regional languages have started their operations. For foreign channels, viewers in India are a prime target. Undoubtedly, these private satellite channels have started their operations purely from the commercial point of view. Since this business of running a private satellite channel requires very high capital investments all-out efforts are made to get as much commercial revenue as possible through advertising. Advertising revenues will grow, and keep growing, only when viewership keeps gorwing, larger and larger. This is ensured by providing entertainment, more entertainment, and more entertainment, 24 hours a day, 365 days a year. Undoubtedly, entertainment of viewers is also important. But so much of importance and all kinds of entertainment? Clean and healthy entertainment programmes are certainly needed but showing of mind-boggling programmes, alien to viewer's culture cannot be the only objective of a powerful medium like television in a developing country like India where several pressing issues need attention and continuous cooperation of media.

Role of Public Service Broadcasting

In this context, another question that needs discussion by this distinguished gathering relates to the role of public service broadcasting television channels like Doordarshan. These channels, in order to face competition from private satellite channels, decided to add heavy doses of entertainment programmes. Directly and indirectly, the contents of these entertainment programmes are dictated by the sponsors and advertisers. Not only that, such programmes are shown at prime-time when the viewership is highest. Public service broadcasting channels do claim that they are showing several other useful, informative, instructional and socially relevant programmes, but at what time and what kind of viewership such programmes command? How far is it justified that the public service broadcasting television channel abdicates its social responsibility? I leave this for you to discuss and show us the way. Let me briefly refer to the situation of television in Germany. Private channels started their programmes in the eighties with precisely the same philosophy as their counterparts all over the world which is making as money as possible.

Based on often cheap serials, sitcoms, an inflation of talkshows and sport events they were able to attract an increasing viewership which went to the detriment of the public channels. Their reaction was very similar to that we witness in India, namely, they tried to sometimes copy the programme structure and contents of the private suppliers. This strategy was far from successful only leading to decreases of both viewership and quality as many viewers opted for the original, the private channels, instead of the copy.

In another strategic turnaround the public channels reconsidered and remembered their strengths which lie in high quality information and self-produced TV films. Thus, they were able to re-attract some of the viewers they had originality lost.

It seems, that a division of labour between private and public channels could emerge in Germany where viewers switch to private channels for light entertainment and to the public television service for news, features and other programmes which contain a relatively high degree of information. Thus, there is even increasing pressure on private channels to improve the quality, particularly of their news services. I feel that similar positive developments might happen in television in India also.

Shift from Information to Infotainment

Coming to the influence of market forces on the press, the issue is as to how far press can allow the business interests overshadow completely the journalistic inputs in the newspapers. Press, being in the private sector, has to depend largely on commercial advertisements to make it a commercially viable proposition. This is quite understandable also. But some of the recent developments in the press world need in-depth discussion in this colloquium. Price-war among major newspapers, intensive publicity campaigns, hardsell techniques, major shift from providing information to focusing on infotainment—all these are a direct result of present market driven media situation. Press has played a very significant role in shaping India's overall development. The present influence of market forces on press needs careful scrutiny. Although, so far I have only touched upon the influence of market forces on television and press in my presentation, a similar situation may arise in the case of a very powerful medium, radio. We may be facing several challenges when radio is privatised in India and the operators would again be guided by the market forces. I am sure that these, and other related issues will be taken up for detailed discussion in this colloquium.

Since we at the FES are committed to the concept and basic values of democratic socialism, I would like to share with you some of the basic principles of the SPD (the Social Democratic Party of Germany) relating to the issue of Market and Control.

While adopting the Basic Policy Programme of the SPD, at the programme conference held in Berlin in December 1989, it was clearly understood that in a democratically established system, the market and competition are indispensable and large number of economic decision making is effectively coordinated through the market. The concept of market and control was explicitly spelt out as follows :

> Economic democracy requires entrepreneurial initiative and performance. We respect this and support this. However, it must also prove itself in its social and ecological responsibility.
> Competition benefits consumers and their free purchasing choice. The market is an instrument for attaining a balance between supply and demand. It is, when embedded in a correspondingly oriented framework, also an efficient instrument for controlling demand and supply. It can provide information on possible economic and structural developments. However, the market can neither bring about full employment nor effect just distribution nor protect the environment.
> Competition as far as possible—planning as far as necessary.

I would like to conclude by touching upon briefly, about the work of the Media and Communication Department in the International Cooperation Division of FES. The Foundation has helped to develop mass communication and media in the Third World countries since the early 1970s. Promotion of media and communication falls within the Foundation's overall belief to promote democratic structures and processes by which it wants to contribute to countries' and region's social, political and economic stability. FES's support in this area is to benefit specially those who have remained underprivileged by existing structures—the economically weaker countries—to strengthen them; the poorer groups in society (e.g. rural people)—to improve their position in it; the trade unions as one of the FES' traditional target groups—to help them assert their demands.

The traditional activities of the media and communication department of FES aim at promoting mass media and information systems in the third world. It includes :

- — News Exchange programmes like ASIAVISION, LATINVISION, ARABVISION and CARIBVISION.
- — International and regional conferences in cooperation with media-relevant organisations at the highest level.
- — Cooperation with institutions in the Third World concerned with scientific research in the field of media and journalistic training.
- — Training and follow-up programmes like seminars, workshops, on-the-job training, consultancy, etc. to be organised in cooperation with individual broadcasting corporations, radio and TV stations and news agencies.

At the moment, FES activities extend to Africa, Asia and the Pacific, Latin America and the Caribbean.

—HORST MUND

COMMERCIALISATION OF MEDIA

1

INFLUENCE OF ADVERTISING ON MEDIA STRUCTURES

—D. K. BOSE

While the creation and existence of any media channel is for the sole purpose of communication, the role of mass-media is very specific. All forms of mass-media must fulfil three basic human needs :

(i) Information
(ii) Knowledge
(iii) Entertainment

Different people at different times have different levels of interest. Because of this phenomenon the rate of growth of different media at different times has varied.

The political and cultural environment have significantly influenced the role and the growth of various mass media. The control of both the form and the content influenced by the state has created structures unsuitable in a changing environment leading to a stunted growth. Cultural influence in the past has primarily affected the content structure depending upon the strengths/weaknesses of that culture. The role or influence of technology and peoples' interest in moulding media structures have become somewhat subservient to market forces with the onset of what is called the "consumer society".

The Consumer Society and Media Structures

The consumer society imposes the market forces in creating and then using media structures and meets its needs.

The consumer society shifts its power base from political

influence to economic influence. The consumer society promotes the use of technology in order to produce a variety of consumables in great numbers and at great speed. The market forces of influence are :

Mass and speciality production,
Large number of producers,
Competitiveness,
Audience segmentation,
Creation of new media,
Changing consumer behaviour, and
Dynamic market economy

Technology and market forces introduced by liberalization affect the way marketing and advertising operate. In fact, the linkages among factors such as product/services, market, audience, media, advertising are so integrated that it is becoming difficult to ascertain who is influencing whom.

There is another way to look at this picture.

Exposure to existing media

↓

Societal changes

↓

New products

↓

Advertising

↓

Creation of new media

Let us at this stage take a look at the changes happening in media and advertising. This will help us understand the new relationships being built.

The last five years have witnessed newspapers go through major changes in widening the readership base. The major changes introduced are colour, special pull outs and supplements, more editions, local editions, etc. The magazines on the other hand have either killed commercially unviable titles or have introduced special interest titles.

Radio has been given a new life with the introduction of FM channels attracting specific and select audience groups.

TV is in the midst of a revolution. Over 50 channels, both national and regional, many of them telecasting 24 hours a day, are now available through terrestrial satellite and cable. Through a population of 50 million sets, the medium of television reaches 6/7 urban households out of ten. In rural areas, one out of every five homes has a TV set. At the touch of a button, the medium has the potential to reach close to 250 million people, a staggering number.

The outdoor medium has witnessed a sea change. From painted boards to bill boards to neon to LED to Vinyl. From front lit to back lit. From three-dimensional to live.

These changes in media were possible through structural changes within the existing ones and through introduction of new ones with new structures. The question really is : how has advertising influenced existing media and how has it created new ones? In both cases, the contribution of advertising has been significant.

One can cite a number of examples but for now I shall take up those that have had the greatest impact. First the print media. Newspapers have introduced colour supplements, weekend supplements, special supplements among other value additions not only to create reader appeal but also to satisfy demanding advertisers. Loss of advertising revenue to television was a major factor that inspired these changes. FMCG advertisers had to be lured back to the newspaper fold. Competition within the newspaper industry was becoming more and more intense. At the same time, the cost of bringing out a newspaper was rising to alarming proportions. While revenue from subscriptions was falling. In these circumstances, dependence on advertising revenue grew. It was a question of survival.

As a result, newspapers witnessed an internal structural change. Interaction between the marketing and editorial functions was now closer than ever before. There was also an external change—in the relationship with advertisers, especially those entering the capital market. Their need was to establish credibility through a presence in the editorial columns. And so, advertisers began to exercise some influence on editorial content and structure.

Magazines have suffered the most. Many have died under the weight of competition and loss of advertising revenue. Those that have survived rely on a vast circulation base. A few have been kept alive by a cash cow in the stable. In recent years, India has seen a proliferation of niche magazines : speciality magazines for women, professional titles, magazines on fashion, magazines for teenagers, magazines on TV programmes, computers, lifestyles, etc. These new channels have created just the right environment in which to speak to focused segments.

The dependence on advertising has increased. Internally, the marketing department exercises greater influence on editorial policy. Externally, the demands of advertisers to share editorial space have increased. Structurally, therefore, editorial is under pressure. This is the trend so far at the infancy of consumerism.

FM Radio

The radio medium has not been affected that significantly. However, there are some structural changes in the management of the medium. These have come about with the introduction of the FM channel that allows private participation, interaction between listener and station/advertiser, flexibility of programme content and focus. Is advertising responsible for this change? Yes, to a great extent. It was advertising that needed to reach out to a new emerging audience segment in a specific media environment. The conventional format did not meet this requirement. FM does.

On FM, it is sometimes difficult to distinguish between editorial and advertising.

The television medium, though introduced in this country around the end of the fifties, opened up to advertising only around 1976. Even after that editorial continued to dominate the medium. Not till July, 1984 did the floodgates open. The first signs of change came in the form of sponsored programmes.

Television was funded by public money. Though it was legislated that money earned by the medium would be ploughed back for its development, unfortunately that was not to be. By 1990/91, its coffers were empty. This was the time when competition arrived in the form of satellite and cable networks.

Doordarshan lost further ground through significant reductions in government funding. This situation compelled Doordarshan to commercialise its Metro Channel. It is inevitable that advertiser supported or sponsored programming will have a natural bias towards audience maximising programme topics and audience maximising treatment to all topics.

Because of the strong structural relationship advertising enjoys with various media, quite often censorship or control cannot fully safeguard programme content and treatment from the influence of advertising.

Another factor that must be borne in mind is that the sole source of income for most Satellite Channels is advertising. Since there will always be a source credibility gap attached to advertising, it will constantly seek some integration with the editorial or in some cases go to an extreme of affecting editorial content and treatment.

In a consumer society, the economic structure itself undergoes a change. This leads to socio-economic changes throwing out old patterns and bringing in new ones. Being an integral part of this socio-economic structure, media and advertising cannot be unaffected. However, having said this, I must also very categorically state that changes creating shock values should be avoided and that can be done only if media acts as a gatekeeper and does not buckle under pressure. Because today's technology is capable of creating media channels which can destroy societies if not handled with care.

2

ADVERTISING AND MARKET-DRIVEN JOURNALISM

—V. S. GUPTA

The most obvious reference to market forces in today's environment is the process of economic liberalisation that the country is witnessing at a very rapid pace. The government, over the last few years from July 1991 onwards introduced a comprehensive economic policy package which focused, among others, on correcting the external value of rupee, delicensing industrial sector, liberalisation and debureaucratising import licensing system.

This process of liberalisation has had an impact on every sphere of commercial activity, and the media industry is no exception. The rapid economic growth has been accompanied by a dramatic increase in advertising. Today billions of dollars are spent on media advertising in Asia, all aimed at enticing the burgeoning middle class, thus encouraging the forces of commercialism and consumerism. The gradual build-up of multinational business activity has resulted in the transformation of consumer behaviour as the region shifts from traditional to mass market and advertising is positioned at the centre of this change.

Emerging Forces of Commercialism and Consumerism

Broadcasting organisations are often caught between the conflicting demands of their sponsors and their audiences. Most of these organisations slowly give way to pressures from their sponsors. Commercialisation of the broadcast media has been viewed with concern all around. As early as November 1974, the

Brazilian Minister of Education had said: Commercial television is imposing on the youngsters and children of our country a culture that has nothing to do with Brazilian culture. . . . Thus, instead of being a creative element in the diffusion of Brazilian culture, television appears as a privileged vehicle of cultural import, a basic factor in the "decharacterization" of our creativity.

Likewise in Indonesia, the government found that television commercials were creating a *consumerist mentality* among its villagers (expressed by sharply increased sales of cigarettes and soft drinks to villages) so in 1981, all commercial advertisements were banned on Indonesian television. While such a step is impossible to contemplate in the Indian situation, the Working Group on Software Planning for Doordarshan (Joshi Committee Report) stressed, as early as 1985, the need to prevent '*the appropriation of television by the emerging forces of commercialism and consumerism*'. While these forces slowly tightened their grip on Doordarshan, liberation came for the Indian T.V. viewers via foreign satellites. The Gulf War in February 1991 ushered in CNN. Subsequently new cable networks sprang up, Satellite Television for the Asian Region (STAR) began operation out of Hong Kong.

India is increasingly becoming the playing field of world's biggest media players for their share of our unregulated 15 million homes Cable TV market run by 60,000 operators. This market is bigger than that of any market in Europe, barring Russia and Germany. Not surprisingly, by mid 1993 India and the market it represented had caught the attention of the world's best known media marauder, Rupert Murdoch. He bought controlling shares in STAR in July 1993 and later, in December that year, 49 per cent of the equity in Zee TV.

Television Advertising

Big money and bigger target audience : Advertisements today seem more capable of swaying the masses than ever before. The Wills World Cup is remembered as much for its nail biting finals, India's incredible debacle at Eden Gardens and Sri Lanka's spectacular victory—as much as for its commercial extravaganza and glitzy advertisements.

The entertaining battle between the Coke and Pepsi almost became bigger than the tussle for the World Cup! Proving that advertising in India has finally gone beyond 'boom time'. *Big money, big advertisements and a bigger target audience than ever before has the ad world on an all time high.* A surfeit of commercials, press campaigns and hoardings combine to form an effective visual onslaught on the senses. We end up becoming willing victims of media's most enticing side—an aggressive, glamorous ad strategy.

Frothy Entertainment, Fun and Frolic

The *Sengupta Committee Report on Prasar Bharati* which submitted its recommendations to the Minister for Information and Broadcasting in August 1996 has pointed out : In the wake of large influx of alien entertainment, directed to *the top crust, the minority with growing purchasing power and propensity to spend, the significance of public service broadcasting needs no over-emphasis*. The high presence of more *frothy entertainment, fun and frolic* can only amuse for a while but cannot meet the real desires of people unless the fare offered is imbued with social purpose. We believe broadcasting has *a higher purpose than the constant drive to reach out to the largest possible number of people*, flattening out in the process disparate audiences into a homogeneous mass of buyers. *Crass commercialisation hinders variety in approach and style, resulting in mere variation of the same theme.*

In a paper, *Advertising in Asia—From Dependence to Convergence*, presented at the *AMIC 25th Anniversary Conference at Singapore held in June 1996*, Katherine Toland Frith, Chair of Advertising, Pennsylvania State University, quoting from Michael Anderson's book, *Madison Avenue in Asia—Politics and Transnational Advertising*, said :

> The impact of the transnational corporations (TNCs) of the needs and aspirations of the Third World masses living amidst scarcity and poverty is not always encouraging.
>
> The consumption gap between the few rich and many poor continues. Progress towards reducing the cultural shock, eliminating poverty and other forms of inequality,

ensuring citizens full participation in their nation's decision making process or fostering national self-reliant action has been slow at best.

Mandi House has tended to allow the dictates of commercialism to adversely affect the content of its telecasts. The ad blitz which has engulfed the channels of Doordarshan has made many worthwhile programmes, serials and films unwatchable. The actual programme being aired often appears almost fleetingly *between waves of commercials*. Sometimes, ads are deliberately inserted to distort and twist programme sequences. This is against all ethics and norms of public or even commercial, telecasting, an unwarranted imposition on viewers. The ads stretch the duration of a film to hours beyond its actual length.

Trivialising Cultural Traditions

Before the disease of privatisation afflicted Doordarshan; programmes were dull but certainly less damaging, at best a waste of a precious national resource. Misconceived privatisation on the other hand has made public broadcasting hostage to crass commercialism. Programmes are not only being drowned in ads but also diverted from the national channels. Doordarshan should develop sensibilities required for public broadcasting which is so far not much in evidence. This is possible only if Doordarshan exploits the advantages of the market instead of becoming its willing victim.

In a seminar organised by AMIC at Kuala Lumpur in August 1995 on, *Asian Values in Journalism*, the Information Minister of Malaysia in his inaugural address, pointed to the several instances where media was responsible for demigrating our cultural traditions. He specifically cited two examples and both the examples were from India. The abusive expression used against Mahatma Gandhi in the STAR television programme hosted by Nikki Bedi; and the newsclip of cows straddling the Bombay streets shown on the occasion of launching of CNN Doordarshan agreement. In both cases sensitivities of the Indian viewers were deeply hurt. These instances were not the only ones which have evoked concern and unhappiness about the values that the Indian television tends to foster. Media analysis and commentators have pointed to country lacking a TV policy which would promote relevant, good quality programmes while discouraging competitive mindlessness and vulgarity.

In this free-for-all scenario, there has been a steady deterioration in the quality of most programmes. The President of the Cable Operators Associations, Roopa Sharma says; she receives more and more complaints about explicitly sexual sequences included in programmes for universal distribution. Most entertainment channels are slaves to glitzy western consumption and sex and violence themes.

Market-Driven Journalism—Let the Citizen Beware

In one of the recent publications titled, "*Market-Driven Journalism—Let the Citizen Beware*", John H. McManus, an Assistant Professor in the Communication Department at Santa Clara University and a former newspaper reporter, points out how the formerly revered practice of news reporting from public interest has been unsurped by *MBA/Corporate-driven* view that the news is a "product" and the reader or reviewer a "customer". The book also studies the way in which media firms deploy resources, such as—reporters or photographers, to maximise return to stock holders and how such practices affect journalistic quality. Given the nature of American culture and its market-based economy, commercial media firms must compete for necessary resources in four markets—one each for investors, sources of news, advertisers and news consumers. The author refers to the advice a prominent news executive gave to the local broadcasters.

A marketing approach demands that we treat a newscast as a consumer durable good, a commodity that a viewer "purchases" by spending time watching it. We must understand that when a viewer watches a specific television programme, the viewer really is spending a precious resource : time. And time for many people is spent as carefully as money.

Having advertising rather than consumers as primary source of income, both for newspapers and television, means that the way to increase profits is to produce a product that has a minimal threshold appeal to the maximum number of "demographically desirable consumers in the signal or circulation area". The economics of newspapers and television favour breadth of appeal over depth.

One of the reasons given as to why local television news falls short of journalistic standard was : Stations are paid for *the size of audience of potential customers they deliver to advertisers*, not on how much viewers learn about current issues and events. So, the decision to seek the largest number of viewers becomes a commercial, not a journalistic one. The public interest is subordinated to the short term interest of advertisers and investors.

The author enlists examples where in market journalism has sought to please more than inform its audience. Across the nation a spate of instances where newspapers omitted reporting critical of powerful advertisers and ran positive content, some of which was composed by advertisers themselves, has been recently reported.

Researcher Steve Singer reported on a national trend towards favourable coverage for automobile advertisers. In some cases newspapers even turned over automotive "news" sections to their advertising departments. Singer quoted Frank Daniels III, executive editor of the once proud News and Observer in Raleigh, NC :

(The auto section is designed) to create a marketplace for advertisers. It doesn't make sense to do it (write critical articles) to piss off advertisers. . . . All this stage, there isn't a single bit of advertising that isn't important. *As a group, auto dealers are our third-largest advertisers.*

Executive editors throughout the country are being trained not to select news of interest to their community as a whole, but only for those people who live in selected neighbourhoods that have certain characteristics wanted by major advertisers.

The practice of selecting news in order to make advertising more effective is becoming so common that it has achieved the status of scientific precision. . . .

The result is the rapidly growing exclusion in standard American newspapers and broadcast operations of the activities and interests of the less affluent and the older people who live in the circulation area.

The impact of market forces, however, is not totally unmitigated; it has its positive aspects as well. The presentations have become slicker and better. The competition has given immense opportunity to improve the contents, quality and appeal of the programmes. In China, in order to survive in market competition, the print based format of broadcasting was discarded and broadcasters are now given greater independence in programming as hosts and anchors. News reporting has become more timely and daring in exposing social problems, while entertainment programmes have also become more lively. More events are now covered live, adding more colour to the overall programming.

Even in these days of Mega Media Mergers, which is catching on in the US and elsewhere very fast, Meheroo Jussawala has given an instance as to how FCC, concerned about educational aspects, made Westinghouse-CBS merger agree to air three hours of educational programming for children every week.

Combating Commercialisation of News and Junk Journalism

In order to combat the rising trend of commercialisation of news, John H. McManus, referred to earlier, has suggested educating journalists to beçome professionals and to instil in students greater sense of professionalism. Ethical standards are inculcated by journalism educators, by professional groups such as the Radio and Television News Directors Association and the Society of Professional Journalists, and by mid-career educational experiences such as the Knight and Nieman fellowships. All are important actions to improve the quality of journalism, but by themselves, they are likely to prove ineffective.

Interestingly the author admits : A reporter or editor in a profit maximizing media firm, who subordinates market standards to those of journalism, may be tolerated about as long as a counter clerk at McDonald's who refuses to sell fried food. There is simply no evidence that professionalism can restrain corporate demands for profit. Bagdikian recently pointed out that American news media have never had better educated or more professional journalists then they have today, *yet bottom-line oriented executives are increasingly moving their organization away from quality journalism.*

Whatever may be the compulsions of catering the interests

of investors and advertisers, efforts to curb junk journalism through an emphasis on professionalisation, both in journalism training and in organisation of reporters and editors should continue.

Increasing public awareness of the consequences of junk journalism may be the surest route to a healthier information diet. There lies some hope in combating the rising influence of market forces on media institutions.

All that I can conclude would be : Society's headlights have to shine faster and more intensely than ever before; their beams must be bright enough for us to see our options, help crystalise our opinions, considerations and consequences more clearly.

REFERENCES

Dre'ze, Jean and Sen, Amartya (1995). *India : Economic Development and Social Opportunity*. Oxford University Press, Bombay.

Frith, Katherine Toland (1996). Advertising in Asia—From Dependence to Convergence. Paper presented at the AMIC 25th Anniversary Conference, 1-3 June 1996, Pan Pacific Hotel, Singapore.

Gupta, V. S. (1995). Influence of Politics and Policies on Journalism Values in Asia. Paper presented at the AMIC Seminar on Asian Values in Journalism, 24-25 August, 1995, Kuala Lumpur, Malaysia.

Jassawala, Meheroo (1996). Media mega mergers catching on. Paper presented at AMIC 25th Anniversary Conference, 1-3 June 1996, Pan Pacific Hotel, Singapore.

McManus, John H. (1996). *Market-driven Journalism—Let the Citizen Beware*. Sage, London.

Ministry of Information & Broadcasting (1996). The Sengupta Committee Report on Prasar Bharati, New Delhi.

Narayanamoorthy, P.V. (1995). Impact of market forces on media management. Paper presented at AMIC India-IIMC-FES Seminar on 'National Media Policy', 10-11 November, New Delhi.

Sharma, Sanjula (1996). Clamouring for attention. *The Hindustan Times*, 6 April, New Delhi.

Teheranian Majid, Farhad Hakimzadeh and Vidale L. Marcello (1977). *Communication Policy for National Development—A Comprehensive Perspective*. Routledge & Kegan Paul, London.

Times of India (1996). Door without Darshan, 12 February.

UNDP (1993). *Human Development Report*. Oxford University Press, Oxford.

Xioming, Hao (1996). The Commercialisation of China's Broadcasting Media : Causes and Consequences. Paper presented at the AMIC 25th Anniversary Conference, 1-3 June 1996, Pan Pacific Hotel, Singapore.

3

EMERGENT COMMUNICATION TECHNOLOGY AND COMMERCIAL PRESSURES

—SUNIL MISRA

In the decade of the Fifties, late Prime Minister Jawahar Lal Nehru was reported to have commented that India was a poor country and that it could not afford the luxury of television. A few years later (1959), experiments with educational television started from Delhi with subsidised equipment from Philips India, and financial help from the UNESCO. Within a year, a number of research studies conclusively proved that the television could be the answer for the problems of reaching educational facilities to the illiterate masses. Today, we know it was not so easy. In 1975, the National Aeronautics and Space Administration (NASA), USA leased to Indian Government its Advanced Technology Satellite (ATS)-6 for one year, free of charges to provide developmental communication support to the people inhabiting the remote and backward regions of the country. Satellite Instructional Television Experiment (SITE) was perhaps the first and an unique experiment in the world, in using the sophisticated communication technology to reach the millions of hithertofore unreached rural people. Within a year again, a large number of research studies showed that the answer to the problems of development and social reforms lay in the use of television. Today we know that it was too optimistic assessment of the potential of the medium.

In 1982, colour transmission was introduced in the country with two main objectives. One to be at par with those countries which had already been using colour technology; and two to use it for development purposes. As one of the important policy makers remarked "when we tell the farmers that the leaves of the trees turn yellow during the autumn, they cannot see the difference on their black and white television sets." Thus, a medium which started colour transmission for social and development communication, succumbed to the pressures and allurement of easy revenue when the flood gates of commercial advertising were opened.

This is not to denigrate the role and importance of technology of mass communication but to bring in sharper focus the difference between potential of a medium and its actual effectiveness in achieving its social and developmental objectives, within the given administrative ethos, the operational realities and the social setting within which programmes are received. World over, scientific innovations and newer technologies have been promoted with laudable social objectives in mind. However, in majority of the cases they fall in the hands of the selected few who can manipulate them in their favour and to their personal advantage. The fact assumes significance particularly in the context of the developing countries where a selected few control all the resources including the mass media of communication. Thus, people get to see and listen only what the media controllers want to show or tell them.

In a country like India, where literacy is estimated to be 60 per cent and therefore, any medium which can transcend the literacy barriers, can be tremendously important. The role of Radio and Television has also to be viewed from the point of those 40 per cent illiterates which in absolute numbers work out to be around 390 millions. However, when the media, inspite of being under the state control, give precedence to commercial interests over their developmental commitments, it merits a critical evaluation. Over the years, specially from the Eighties, both radio and television have tried to boost up their revenues from the commercial sources. Tacit encouragement in this appears to have come from the Ministry itself. It is ironical that the two media which were started with the objectives of social transformation and amelioration of the millions of down trodden, have to liaise with the promoters of consumer goods. It is noteworthy in this context that a Non-lapseable Fund (NLF) was started to pool in commercial revenue and use it for the development and expansion of Akashvani and Doordarshan. In a way, it meant that to be able to develop and expand as a medium for public service, these media had to earn revenue from not so public service oriented sources.

In the field of television transmission, all the available channels, except Doordarshan to an extent, have come to be dominated by monopolistic organisations for whom perhaps public service ranks lowest in order of priority. It is a well documented fact that when an alternative is available to the audiences in the form of light entertainment programmes, they would prefer to shift from the serious programmes. Thus, in order to attract greater number of viewers and thereby rake in profits from commercial advertisements, most of the channels are competing in presenting programmes which only cater to the popular tastes. As Bhaskar Rao remarked "Media have become less programme men oriented and more Manager driven." In this process, television channels are aiming for "captive audience and passive viewer," than for "active and enlightened citizens."

This is the age of revolution in the information technology. The imperative need is to make conscious efforts to keep pace with it. The technology is there and one cannot simply wish it away. Therefore, the need is to plan for its proper use towards amelioration and development of the socially and economically underprivileged sections of the society; also to create conditions for better utilisation of social, civic, scientific and development oriented services.

The emergent communication technology and the resultant commercial pressures raise certain basic issues which merit a mention at this stage.

1. In the wake of revolution in the information technology, perspective planning is called for to evolve suitable policies, develop appropriate systems and think of regulatory mechanisms to be able to fully exploit the potential of the new technology for public service.
2. In order to raise their earnings, the state owned media appear to be joining the race for generating commercial revenue. In the process, they have lost their own identity; particularly, the television has come to be recognised as purely a medium of entertainment. This has, to an extent, reduced its effectiveness as a medium

of development. Can the government not provide financial support for Akashvani and Doordarshan to enable them pursue the basic roles and responsibilities as indicated in their motto of "Satyam Shivam Sundaram", and "Bahujan Hitai—Bahujan Sukhai", should the two media continue to rely on commercial revenue for additional resource generation.

3. In order to be able to serve the masses, the media have to know about people's expectations, aspirations and the information needs. But this seems to be a neglected area. Without a strong research and feed-back support, the media will not be able to provide target group and need specific information which is the key to effective communication.

4

COMMERCIALISATION OF MEDIA INSTITUTIONS
Facing the Challenge

—VIR BALA AGGARWAL

During the recent years, India—alongwith the rest of the world—has witnessed a rapid, almost mind boggling proliferation of new information and media technologies so much so that there have been profound and fundamental changes in almost every sphere of human activity—life styles, entertainment, work culture, modes of communication and above all, social and cultural values in the society.

The phenomenal expansion of mass media, telecommunication and advertising industry during the past decade in the world, more so in India since the policy of liberalisation was ushered in 1991, and their socio-cultural impact, have been a subject matter of discussion and deep concern at various levels in numerous conferences and seminars.

That the forces of commercialism and consumerism are marching ahead relentlessly and the concern has been so deep is clear from the opening sentence of the Introduction to the latest book—The Impact of Television Advertising on Children by Namita Unnikrishnan and Shailaja Bajpai. The authors in the opening sentence of the Introduction say : This book is the result of a growing sense of unease at what has been happening in the world of television and the manner in which ideas conveyed by television, particularly TV advertising, are beginning to shape our consciousness.

This deep concern is clearly visible throughout the research study, the first of its kind pertaining to India. There have also been a spate of editorials and articles on the adverse impact of advertising and the trend of consumerism developing fast in the urban society in general and the children in particular. The Introduction (in the above book) concludes :

> Culturally, we found that TV advertising is imposing an image of life that is completely alien to the vast majority of Indian children. Many children are beginning to believe that the India and the Indians they see in TV ads are the only ones worth emulating and learning from. In other words, all other Indians and Indian lifestyles are either retrograde or passe—may be even both.
>
> Unfortunately, few attempts are being made to draw children, or adults for that matter, into a critical debate on the values and lifestyles that television and the advertising on it advocate. As a result, material aspira-tions are reaching unrealistic heights. Development has never appeared so disjointed. While consumerism is spreading like wildfire, access to the basics of life remains a serious problem for many.

If the sense of unease and concern with the trend of cultural alienation and inculcation of western values in the society is deep and pervasive; equally strong is the disquiet over the growing influence of multinationals and market forces on the media institutions in the country. The newly emerging technologies are all capital intensive and bring with them value system and other attributes associated with the culture of their countries. A genuine fear exists that the media depends on advertising for survival, which in turn obeys the dictates of the tiny community of big business houses and corporations.

Pointing out to the dangers of inculcating the wrong value system amongst the audience; Unnikrishnan and Bajpai point out

> As a powerful influencer, television serves the interests of this tiny community by spreading their messages far and wide and thereby enabling them to consolidate their hold. As Jerry Mander has said :
>
> "The spread of television unified a whole people within a

> system of conceptions and living patterns that made possible the expansion of huge economic enterprise. Because of it, our whole culture and the physical shape of the environment, no more or less than our minds and feelings, have been computerised, linearised, sub-urbanised and packaged for sale."

Quality of TV Programmes

It was indeed startling to know that the Chairman of the National Human Rights Commission, Mr. Justice Ranganath Mishra sought the support of the United Nations in dealing with violence on television. Speaking on the activities of the Commission at the Centre for Strategic and International Studies in Washington, Mr. Mishra said that he had written to the US Secretary General, Mr. Ghali on the subject of violence on television which militated against the concept of human rights. He said his commission was trying to stop projection of violence on the Indian television but foreign television shows, now available in the country, depicted violence in a big way.

Ethics in Business Journalism and Manipulative and Market Forces

If the quality of television programmes, under advertising pressures, has been debased; journalists in print media, particularly those in business journalism have come in for attention for accepting envelopes containing gift coupons or hard cash at press conferences where new issues are launched.

Writing in the *Tribune* `Strange Results of Liberalisation`, one of the eminent columnists M. V. Kamath says : What journalists should be concerned about is the corruption of their brethren on a scale that is mind boggling. Giving a graphic account of the process of cash collection in a day in the life of a reporter, Kamath also points to an other aspect of the problem—Conformity. Does that mean there are no honest journalists in the profession. The issue is not honesty but conformity. If the honest journalist refuses to accept the gifts given to him, he falls foul of his colleagues. Every one accepts gifts. That is the done thing.

Of late the concept being promoted is that selling newspapers is just like selling cakes of soap. The newspaper is a product and the emphasis is on packaging. The commercial and the business side, modern management methods and techniques, contract journalism, loss of authority of the editor to proprietor are some of the issues currently being confronted. Does an editor's freedom end where the proprietor's eyebrows begin to rise? Is an editor, the custodian of the proprietor's vested interest?, asks the media educator, P. N. Malhan and says : The value of the newspaper is of its contents, the selection of which is the responsibility of the editor.

The present position, according to S. Nihal Singh is : It is true that the traditional concept of the editor of a major established English language newspaper was of a man in an ivory tower disdainful of commerce and the lowly tasks carried out by advertisement and other managers. There was little interaction between such an editor and his circulation manager. The pendulum now seems to have swung to the other extreme in some newspaper establishments. The editor has become a non-entity. The proprietor and his managers lay down the law and enjoy bigger salaries and perquisites than members of the editorial staff.

Public Service Broadcasting

Public service advertising or features have not yet surfaced in the Indian media. As in the case in Japan, US and other countries where large corporations produce features on cancer, AIDS, physical fitness programmes, nutrition, immunising and other social beneficial measures through social marketing of ideas. Alongwith the liberalisation of the media, the market forces should be attentive to these aspects of the human society in India. Otherwise, we will continue to have a hiatus between consuming classes and the deprived classes which will not be a healthy development for developing countries. Likewise, the media should step out beyond limits of urban middle class and enter the vast rural population in the country which account for nearly 60 per cent of India's population. A country like China has been able to do this and invite foreign investments. Ethical choices have still to be made by media gate-keepers who shape the minds, attitudes and opinions of the people. A certain amount of conflict and social grievance, part of any growth oriented society and our media should not gloss over these social aspects of governance. Instead, it should discover root causes and suggest remedies. Though profit is legitimate form of running a business; alongwith profit, there are also social accountability and public interest considerations. It is here that market forces can give a new direction and probably new guidelines, to counter the forces of unbridled consumerism which have been promoted in the first flush of liberalisation.

The search for solution is not easy. One thing, however, is apparent—we would need more concerted efforts, more research studies and advocacy groups to create a body of public opinion against the rapid onslaught of the commercialisation of media institutions in the country. Equally important would be policy initiatives at the national level which could take note of the concerns being articulated through the non-governmental organisations, public fora and other such bodies/organizations.

REFERENCES

Gupta, V. S. and Aggarwal, Vir Bala (1996). *Media Policy and Nation Building.* Concept Publishing Company, New Delhi.

Narayanamoorthy, P. V. (1995). Impact of market forces on media management. Paper presented at AMIC India-IIMC-FES Seminar on `National Media Policy`, 10-11 Nov., New Delhi.

Ninan Sevanti (1995). *Through the Magic Window - Television and Change in India.* Penguin Books, India, New Delhi.

Narayanan, V. N. (1996). *Hindustan Times*, What the papers do not say, 25 August.

S. Nihal Singh (1992). *Your Slip is Showing*, Indian Press Today, UBS Publishers, New Delhi.

Unnikrishnan Namita and Bajpai Shailaja (1996). *The Impact of Television Advertising on Children*, Sage, New Delhi.

5

DISINFORMATION AND MARKET FORCES

—P. P. GHOSH

The relevance of the market forces for the media is not a new phenomenon. Even before, a large part of the print media, films and some of the performing arts was influenced by market forces, some of them even greatly. What is, however, new in this context is that the market forces are no longer just one of several other relevant factors, but has almost become the only relevant factor in deciding the relative size of different forms of media as well as their content. This increasing compulsion of the media to submit itself completely to the forces of the market is possibly the issue that is confronting us today. The obvious concern is about possible extinction of those forms and contents of media which are unable to meet the criterion of market forces but are of undoubted relevance towards creation of a better society, and the possible expansion of those parts of media which clearly harms the general societal interest, but are able to sustain itself because a section of the society finds it profitable in an economic sense to support it through, of course, the market mechanism.

Part of the change in this relation between market and media, it should be noted, is because the ascendance of the concept of market to a status where it is seen almost as an ideology. But that is not the only factor. The media itself, viewed as an economic activity which disseminates information, has also undergone radical changes causing a much larger role of the market forces in its affairs. The most fundamental aspect of this change in the character of the media is that previously, information was perceived as a source of knowledge, wisdom and enlightenment. In today's world, besides those, information is also a source of 'power'—an institution which has more information about others is in a position to manoeuver and manipulate and, hence, more powerful. This power implication of information is what lends it a character of a commodity, commanding a price which may or may not reflect its value.

Another important dimension of information as a commodity is that disinformation is also a commodity and media is a vehicle for both. Just as information makes an individual or organisation potentially more powerful, by being innocently fed with disinformation it can become vulnerable. A very strong example of the power of disinformation is the content of political news which quite often consists of incomplete and selective truth. The field of advertising is yet another example where persistent disinformation is able to produce a distorted preference pattern among the consumers, serving the interest of the giant producers. Indeed, producers now need not produce what the consumers want, but the latter can be made to want what the producers produce. Such being the power of information or disinformation, it is very natural that the entire media space is under pressure and it thus yields easily to the market forces. Space is allocated to those messages which are paid for; other messages, howsoever desirable, are either altogether neglected or are reluctantly given a little space just to avoid the criticism that media is 'wholly' a commercial activity.

Yet another phenomenon which has caused a major change in the character of relation between the media and market is the technological base of the media. The new technology based on satellites, computers, etc. not only makes the storage, processing and transmission of information much easier, but it does so at a much reduced cost. Because of such cost reduction, information management or media is now attracting more attention as a commercial activity, relegating many of its non-commercial dimensions to the background.

The fact that many of the changes that have taken place in the context of media-market relation is because of certain changes in the media itself, as discussed before, should not lead one to ignore the other complementary factor that market mechanism itself is now being projected as a nearly flawless mechanism not only for establishing an economic equilibrium, but even for deciding the social issues. This is obviously an ideological issue. But when protagonists of the market try to settle the question by quoting Adam Smith that the most trusted mechanism for ensuring the greatest good of the greatest number is the invisible hand of the market mechanism, they obviously ignore that, among other things, the argument overlooks the clear difference between the two markets —one of now and other of two hundred years ago. The invisible hands of Adam Smith was that of a young market after capitalist development had just started in England; but in complete contrast, today`s invisible hands are that of a larger, stronger and globalised market. To assume that these hands are as unerring as they were two centuries ago is both unsafe and unwise.

SOCIAL RESPONSIBILITY OF MEDIA

6

EMERGING MARKET FORCES AND SOCIAL RESPONSIBILITY OF MEDIA

—AJIT BHATTACHARJEA

One of the most disturbing developments in recent years is the apprehension that the media is spinning out of control, that it is being blown whichever way the winds of consumerism and globalism take it. The feeling stems primarily from the impact of satellite television, with its ever-multiplying number of channels, subject to no national or international control mechanism. Some of the programmes we are now able to see are outstanding, but many of them depend on increasing doses of sex and violence to attract viewership.

Projection of sex and violence is not new to India. Cinema films have exploited such scenes for years. But access to cinemas is limited, with children kept out of adult films. Inability to read also keeps them out of the reach of pornography until they are somewhat older. On the other hand, TV enters the living room directly; its images have greater impact on the very young who cannot distinguish fact from fiction. Children and teenagers cannot be banned from watching, while their elders do so. It is not only sex and violence that affect them; they are dazzled by the attractive portrayal of western cultures and lose respect for their own. This shows in changes of speech, dress, food habits, even the way they address their elders. They are also sensitised to the culture of the commercials that follow programmes. The overall result is that children are becoming precocious, demanding and alienated from traditional norms and culture.

A recent book on the impact of television and TV advertising on Indian children by Namita Unnikrishnan and Shailaja

Bajpai provides researched data on how much it distorts their lives and values. What they view on the TV screen becomes reality for them. This includes the sex-oriented life-styles projected daily by American soap operas like The Bold and the Beautiful and Santa Barbara. Commercials often focus on children and make them judge themselves and their peers by their access to advertised goods.

The line between entertainment and news is disappearing. So-called live documentaries and news coverage are often staged in advance. Scenes are superimposed or separated; others are inserted. Even BBC has been caught out inserting visuals from one place into an event in quite a different location. Usually, the change is so expertly handled that the viewer is none the wiser. Then, standby visuals are repeatedly used to fill blanks. They tend to repeat the most violent episodes, thus creating an impression of continuing tension though the tension may be easing. This has been noticeable in the coverage of unrest in Chechnya and Kashmir. Remote locations are preferred. This furthers the impression of an uncivilised world outside the West.

The 1980s saw much debate on the one-sided flow of information between the West and the rest of the world. It was provoked by the MacBride Commission Report, commissioned by UNESCO. Though the degree of inequality has increased with satellite TV, we hear little protest today. While it would be far from correct to suggest that news despatches from western correspondents are consciously biased, differences in culture and political background do influence the presentation of news, often involuntarily. When Kabul fell to the Taliban, for instance, an American reporter suggested that order was being restored to the city, thus giving a degree of legitimacy to the Taliban occupation, which was in line with US policy. This does not imply that indigenous reporters are more objective; only that their biases are more in tune with domestic culture and concerns.

Before the MacBride Commission met, world communications were seen as beneficial to all; it was an innocuous non-controversial subject. The Commission Report raised fundamental questions concerning sources, bias, commercialisation, dominance, above all the political use of information, as this extract indicates : "Communication can be an instrument of power, a revolutionary weapon, a commercial product, or a means of education; it can serve the end either of liberation or oppression, either of the growth of the individual personality or of drilling human beings into conformity."

Mr. Amadou-Mahtar M`Bow, the controversial Director-General of UNESCO who appointed the MacBride Commission, represented the temper of the times. An extended quotation from one of his speeches shows that his views are still relevant, but seldom expressed today. Referring to western media, he said : "With regard to content, the mass media of these countries tend, in the opinion of Third World countries, to emphasise points of view, areas of interest, types of questions and ways of presenting the facts, which all reflect the values of the culture in which they originate.

The information they give out gives special prominence to events for their shock value—to news likely to arouse the public`s interest through surprise, or sometimes provocation, or even scandal. When covering current affairs in the Third World, for example, they seldom probe deeply into the problems arising there, and only occasionally seek to show them in a true light or to discover the real hopes and disappointments of those who are grappling with them.

They measure success or failure, advances and setbacks, by their own criteria, without reference to the history of the peoples concerned, disregarding the constraints that weigh upon them as a result of the present world order. Their attention is more easily drawn to sensational disasters or the witticisms of some publicity—seeking leader than to the desperate efforts of whole peoples to escape from the crushing poverty that affects so many of them. They mete out praise or blame according to whether those concerned share their point of view or reject it. They state facts without any explanation and thus perpetuate prejudices that date back to colonial times."

Western and Indian News Values

There are exceptions today to Mr. M`Bows indictment. Indeed, a few foreign papers cover the rural scene in India better than our own. Where Mr. M`Bow went wrong was to assume that national papers would be less sensation-oriented than the western, or take the trouble to explain the background of events. In fact, there is little to choose between western and Indian news values. This is because readers, everywhere, prefer surprise and provocation to education. Which is why institutions, like the Non-Aligned News Pool, set up in an attempt to balance one-sided news flows, failed to take off.

But Mr. M'Bow's emphasis on the influence of cultural differences on communication is truer now than before satellite television invaded our homes. Yet there is no Third World outcry comparable to that raised at the time. It would seem tha' having been weakened by accepting the economic penetration inherent in the global market system, we have no strength left to resist penetration on the cultural and communication fronts.

Impact of Market Forces on Print Media

The impact of market forces on the print media is not so obvious as on the visual media because it is less direct. But the marked increase in advertising has changed the size, if not the appearance to the same extent, of newspapers. This has had positive as well as negative consequences. Extra pages enable papers to devote special pages to subjects that they had largely ignored before; among them, environment, health, science, gender, law and media itself. Magazine pages cover a wide range of family events.

Salaries have risen in keeping with the market psychology, though this has meant that journalists are tempted to move repeatedly and do not stay long enough in one paper to learn or respect it as an institution. More funds are available for foreign and special assignments, but managements usually prefer to divert them into profits.

The negative impact of market forces on the press is more serious, if less immediately obvious to the reader. The sharp increase in the profitability of the newspaper business—due to the new technology and more advertisements—has made them a good investment. A new breed of owner-editors has produced newspapers, often printed in several locations, at minimum journalistic cost. They have little knowledge of professional values and often do not hesitate to exacerbate communal and caste tensions to increase their circulations, as the Press Council of India has repeatedly found.

The older, well-established papers have also been affected.

The accent on profitability and marketing has meant that the authority of editors has been eroded and they have to defer to managers. Some papers, like the *Times of India*, have no editor at all. They have different editors for different jobs, with managers calling the shots. Since managers are concerned with profits rather than social responsibility, a fall in standards is inevitable, as already evident in the newer owner-editor papers. Managers have little respect for institutions, unless they make money. Here, too, the proprietors of the *Times of India*, Bennet Coleman and Co. have shown the way by shutting down the more than century old *Illustrated Weekly of India*, followed by several other journals that had made a name for themselves, like *Dharmayug* and *Science Today*.

Can anything be done to maintain professional standards and protect viewers and readers from the negative impact of market forces? Judging by its inaction so far, the government is unlikely to do anything to modify the programmes telecast via satellite. Several governments, notably in South-East Asia, have imposed controls on dish antennae and cable networks. There is a danger that such curbs may be used for political censorship. But this could be avoided if an independent body of sociologists and media experts was appointed for the purpose.

We have been following the campaign for Right to Information from government departments with interest since it will enable the media to have access to facts affecting the public. The government is committed to such a measure. The media would benefit equally, if not more, if the measure assured public access to the inner working of media organisations as well. The working of the mass media is of no less importance to the public than that of various government departments. Transparency might help to ensure, for instance, that money was not transferred from the news operations of these organisations to other purposes. A certain minimum of the overall expenses could then be prescribed for news and information.

Some such measures must be taken early if the media is to retain a sense of social responsibility under the pressure of market forces.

7

MEDIA COMMERCIALISATION
Looking Beyond Survival

—UPENDRA VAJPEYI

All revolutions are aimed at rectifying the social aberrations. At the same time, all revolutions have been known to carry in their womb the seeds of fresh disparities eventually culminating into another revolution of uncertain dimensions. The Information Revolution we are witnessing today is no exception to this phenomenon. Even before it has taken full shape, its fallouts are visible.

As we know, it is technological explosion which has brought about the Information Revolution with Media as its principal weapon. Free flow of information acquired a new significance after the second world war when the United Nations and its other agencies sought to emphasize that it was an integral part of civilization, culture and peaceful co-existence. Article 19 of the Universal Declaration of Human Rights laid down "Every one has the right to freedom of opinion and expression. This right includes freedom to hold opinions without interference and to seek, receive and impart information and ideas through any media and regardless of frontiers".

The governments of most countries had appended their signatures to this document—the UN Declaration of Human Rights—as a ritual. And yet none of them was keen to translate it in letter and spirit-for the simple reason that all governments including those which had come into existence after fighting colonialism and authoritarianism, were inclined to believe that information is primarily a prerogative of the rulers. The ruled were entitled to receive only as much information as was doled out to them.

Decentralisation of Electronic Media

I would like to divulge an interesting episode to my friends here. As a part of its ongoing programme for interaction of journalists with different peer groups, especially the people in the government, the National Media Centre organized a convention here in Vigyan Bhavan on Right to Know in 1983. The chief guest in one of the sessions was Mr. Arjun Singh, then Chief Minister of Madhya Pradesh. In his address, one of the suggestions he made was that the Union Government should allow his State to run at its own expense a separate radio channel so that it could provide information to the people of the State in their own language. Mr. Arjun Singh pointed out that Madhya Pradesh was the largest State in size and nearly one-third of its population was tribal, speaking a number of dialects. The centrally organized programmes of radio were unable to render service to the different linguistic groups of his large population. After the convention, we took up the matter with the Union Government on behalf of Madhya Pradesh, hoping that the electronic media may be decentralised in all the States to the advantage of the underprivileged sections which were largely cut off from the information network of any kind.

Not knowing what was in store for him when there would be invasion from the sky and the provisions of the Constitution giving absolute power to the Centre in respect of radio and television, will be blown over without the knowledge and permission of any authority, the then Information and Broadcasting Minister, Mr. H. K. L. Bhagat wrote back after several weeks that the matter had been examined in depth. Madhya Pradesh was being adequately served by AIR. No separate channel for the State was called for.

If we examine the situation in the context of today's discourse, it is the other way now. The process has reversed. The all powerful Government of India is helpless. Far from any control on it, it is unable to arrest the negative features of the dissemination of messages from sky. Perhaps, a more distressing aspect of the government controlled Akashvani and Doordarshan is that it has entered the rat race of the Market Forces, another name of commercialism and subordination of cultural values we claim to preserve.

It may sound offensive to the policy makers who are currently fighting for their own survival that the widest and most effective media under their control is being used as surrogate mother for dumping unpresentable programmes devoid of information, education or even entertainment in the real sense of the term. It is engaged in titilating popular sensualities to save itself from being crowded out from the market. In a way, the State is becoming a victim of its own acts of omission and commission. To resolve the conflict between immediate gain and future uncertainty, the option is exercised in favour of immediate gain derived from all sorts of commercials and programmes irrespective of their malignant influence on impressionable minds.

It is not suggested that there are no healthy programmes on radio or Doordarshan. But, their percentage is declining and their priorities are getting downgraded.

Reaching the Unreached

Secondly, we have to examine our projections in terms of the beneficiaries. The radio covers roughly 95 per cent of population. What about the remaining five per cent? They are certainly not among those who have access to television or print media. How are we going to reach them? The television has certain inherent infirmities. It can be functional only if power supply is available. I do not know if battery operated sets are in the market anywhere. Against an estimated 155 million families, the number of TV sets in India may have reached the figure of 27 million or so. The radio coverage is of the order of 110 million. Evidently, 45 million are still out of the reach of radio and 128 million outside the domain of television. The print media covers hardly 25 per cent of population. The reasons for slow expansion of print media are very many— illiteracy, poverty, lack of communications and concentration of newspaper proprietors in the cities.

Market forces have their own positive role to play in dissemination of information and social interaction. But, the "part" should not become bigger than the "whole". The Information based power structure emerging as the most potent factor in determining all other parameters, it may be suicidal to surrender the media to the market forces. Just as the size of the country did not deter the small number of British traders to capture it politically, the size and population of the country will not prevent the international information operators from overpowering any country without formally capturing it. The methodology of colonization undergoes change according to the capability of the instrument.

Both within and outside the country, the multi-media resources are overtaking the conventional weapons which are likely to become outdated not in very distant future.

Let us, therefore, ask these questions to ourselves :

(1) What is the range of our information network? Is there an obligation of the State to cover the entire population?

(2) (a) How far the market forces are determining the range, quantum and quality of such information?

(b) Is the impact of market forces on the channels of information—both in print and electronic Media—causing distortions in the value system? If so, is it possible to arrest such distortions?

(3) Has the Editor been overtaken by the commercial interests of the Media? If so, how far a free and fearless Media still remains socially accountable?

There is a shloka in Bhagwadgita :

यदयदाचरित श्रेष्ठस्तत्तद्देवेतरो जनः ।
स यत्प्रमाणं कुरुते लोकस्तदनुवर्त्तते ।।

The essence of this is that the leadership of a society sets the precedents/standards which are followed by the rest of the people.

Perhaps, at the policy planning level, we need superior statesmen who will infuse institutions with values and character and who will like to celebrate something more than their own survival.

8

SOCIAL RESPONSIBILITY OF MEDIA FOR RURAL DEVELOPMENT

—B. S. HANSRA AND K. VIJAYARAGHAVAN

Globally, today, the life of man and the society in which he lives has witnessed media and communication explosion. The satellite TV, cable TV, electronic broadcasting and news reading on the screen has come in the homes, this resulted into the greatest change in the living style and the approach to life of people. As a matter of fact, the psychology of people has changed. It is also a fact that this media explosion has affected the minds of our young boys and girls.

Today we live in the age of information. The role of mass media has multiplied in recent times. At present television in India covers 86 per cent of population, whereas radio covers 97 per cent of population. There has been phenomenal increase in the rate of adoption of mass media by Indian households. As against almost 0.0 percentage of adoption of these media in 1945, the adoption of radio in 1990 was 24 per cent, television was 15 per cent, telephones 4 per cent and VCRs 1 per cent. By the 2000 AD, India is expected to have 63 million television sets with an estimated 378 million television viewers (Singhal and Rogers, 1989). Since 1980s the VCR diffused rapidly in India. Today India has an estimated 2.2 million VCRs. India has about 25000 newspapers, magazines and periodicals which includes 2100 dailies. The combined circulation of all these papers and periodicals has been estimated to be about 65 million copies.

With the ever-increasing communication technology, the man and the society in which he lives, has both the intrinsic benefits and the inherent dangers. The space communication satellite systems are capable of transmitting simultaneously to every part of the world, capable also of linking every home and every office in the world of telegraph and telephone. Computers, video telephones, electronic mail, magazine and newspaper delivery and the subscriber will be able to transmit as well as receive information. There will be freedom of choice in viewing whether individually or as a family and for reading one decides what books he will read and when. It is expected that satellite will eventually become only a link in the complex communications networks of the public information system.

Despite its rapid development of communication technology, it still is costly, complex, difficult to operate and more difficult to maintain.

Indian Agricultural Scenario

The Indian agricultural scenario indicates that there are three types of agriculture : commercial, green revolution, and complex, diverse and risk-prone (CDR). The commercial and green revolution agriculture are capitalized family farms/plantations, very high/high use of purchased inputs, relatively uniform environmental conditions, and production stability with moderate risk. The CDR agriculture is mostly practised in rainfed areas by small and poor farmers with low purchased inputs where the farming systems are relatively complex with high environmental diversity and high risk of production stability. There are variations in the physical, social and economic conditions among these three types.

Emerging Picture

An analysis of emerging scenario of media reveals that the media have paid greater attention to politics, entertainment, violence, commercial gain and other related urban interests. The attention paid to rural peoples' interests as well as rural development need is very meagre. Though the electronic media such as radio and TV were introduced in India with the policy objective of promoting agricultural and rural development, disseminating improved farm and home practices, over the years the percentage of time and space devoted to this objective has drastically come down. If the media have to positively respond to the needs of rural people, attention has to be paid to solve problems of rural development.

Some of the measures which can help towards this end are as follows :

I. More Time and Space in Media to be Devoted for Rural Development

The main objective of mass media in these days seems to be to increase readership/viewership so that revenue through advertisements could be increased. As a result entertainment programmes dominate the media and the responsibility of media in promoting rural development has been ignored. The market-driven media is unable to cater to the needs of rural people. If media have to have a positive impact on increasing welfare of rural masses we should have 'market-driving' media instead of 'market-driven' media. This means that media should realise their responsibility in promoting rural development. This calls for devoting more time and space for programmes related to agriculture, animal husbandry, health, sanitation, etc. At least 10 to 15 per cent of time and space has to be devoted for rural development. At present only negligible time and space is provided for this purpose.

There is no doubt that more developmental information is generated now than even before. Even the infrastructural facilities to develop, process and transfer the developmental information have increased manifold. However, the media and information revolution have only opened a great charm in the society particularly in rural areas. There is one small group of information 'haves' and a larger population of 'have nots'. This is due to the fact that increasingly information is regarded as a commodity and it is neatly packed and sold for a price. Media in general are not concerned for the developmental interests and needs of poor mass of rural areas who have less access and purchasing power to get these commodities. This calls for responsibility of media to reach the poorest segment of society with developmental information, so as to reduce the gap between information 'have' and 'have nots'.

II. Separate Television Channel for Agricultural and Rural Development Programmes

As pointed out earlier television was introduced in our country with the main objective of reaching farmers with modern farm technologies. The television which was started with the development objective has fallen prey to market-driven forces resulting in opening separate channels for entertainments, sports, etc. However, the needs of 70 per cent of population in India which depends upon agriculture have been ignored. It is high time that we give more importance to developmental commitments rather than commercial interests. This can be achieved by opening a separate television channel exclusively for agricultural and rural developmental programmes. Recently, the Prime Minister of India has announced the Government's decision to open a separate channel in Doordarshan for agricultural programmes. We hope that this decision will be faithfully implemented so as to meet the developmental needs of majority population of our country.

III. Discouraging the Promotion of Values on Consumerism

The commercial advertising through media has not only created 'consumerist mentality' among urban population but also among rural population. Further studies have revealed that television viewing has resulted in reduction of social interaction, breaking off from traditional norms and distortion of social values. Though it is not possible to ban all commercial advertisements, awareness has to be created among rural people about all ill-effects of media and to guard against the consumerist-mentality. The media should restraint themselves from exploiting public through commercial advertising for the sake of monetary profits.

IV. Developing Entrepreneurial Motivation among Rural Youth

The problem of unemployment among rural youth is well known to us. Instead of taking the youth to a imaginary world of unreality through programmes loaded with sex, violence, etc. the media can play a positive role in solving their practical problem of unemployment. This can be achieved through programmes specifically designed to increase their entrepreneurial motivation and skill, which will increase their overall entrepreneurial competencies and to go in for agro-based self-employment.

V. Creating Awareness on Environmental Protection and Sustainable Development

Due to inputs intensive modern chemical based technologies,

natural resources such as land and water are being degraded. A vast area of land has also been converted to non-farm use. Further biodiversity and ecosystems are destroyed. Today we also face problems due to pollution because of excess use of pesticides and fertilisers. Attempts are being made to promote ecologically sound and sustainable farm technologies. In this context media can play an important role in creating awareness about environmental problems and to promote ecologically sound technologies. The alternative approaches to agricultural production such as low external input and sustainable agriculture, organic farming, biological farming and permaculture have to be promoted.

The media should pay a special attention to the traditional wisdom and informal research undertaken for farmers and rural artisans. Farmers do not accept the technology passively. They make suitable changes and modifications to suit their local conditions. This covers areas like varietal selection, multiple cropping, inter-cropping, irrigation techniques, engineering research, post-harvest technology, etc. The improved methods of farming based on farmer's R and D can be easily accepted and adopted by majority of farming community.

VI. Creating Awareness about Developmental Programmes of Government

Many research studies have pointed out that lack of awareness about governmental development programmes as well as existing facilities is one of the most important reasons for non-participation in the programmes. Awareness about different programmes can be created among poor sections of rural society through media.

VII. Promotion of Rural Newspapers and Journals

Most of the newspapers and journals are published from cities and cater to the needs of urban mass. These publications contain little contents reflecting the interests, values and culture of rural people. Encouragement has to be given to publish local rural newspapers and journals edited and published by rural people who can provide a richer and interesting information related to needs of rural people.

VIII. Focus on Rural Women

Women constitute almost half of the total population and generally live under lower social and economic status. The condition of rural women is still critical who have been treated unequally and unjustly. The rural women contribute greatly towards farm production. However, so far not much attention has been paid to the developmental needs of rural women. The electronic media can make a great impact towards developmental needs of rural women through programmes oriented towards women.

REFERENCE

Singhal, A. and E. M. Rogers (1989). *India's Information Revolution*. Sage Publications, New Delhi.

9

COMMUNITY MEDIA
Challenges and Possibilities

—FRANK KRISHNER

The Indian economy has been going through major changes since 1991. This metamorphosis is referred to as the economic reform process. A major dimension of this process has been the *relaxation of controls* which had earlier governed economic activity such as investment, manufacturing and trade, and the *reduction of public investment* in the industrial sector, infrastructure building and delivery of social services.

For those in the media, there have been several implications. Communications apparatus is increasingly being regarded as the means for private producers to market goods and services. Newspapers have become "market friendly". Privately owned telecommunication and broadcasting services have emerged. Even the state run radio and television networks are being influenced by the market forces. Liberalisation has also led, under a certain combination of circumstances, to the creation of greater pressures on the rural and urban poor.

The development of electronic media in India has been so rapid that we did not have the time, as it were, to fully master the existing modes of communication in the service of development. Like many other developing countries, India was pulled and pushed to adopt the latest technologies. Now, hurled into the arena of satellite television, mega newspaper networks, cyberspace. . . our mainstream media flows towards the consumer. As for those without the means to subsist, they may well be left to look after themselves. The situation was and remains acute in a scenario of so-called development where resources, human and pecuniary, are limited.

There are a lot of voices raised over the so-called consumerist thrust now evident in the mainstream media. Quite a few NGO's are not at all happy with this economic liberalisation that demands a thorough reorientation of "official" priorities. The velocity of changes in technology is so fast that today's technology may become obsolete tomorrow. If the Indian media does not keep abreast with this pace it will struggle along in the competitive world. Rather than winning out on the amount of advertising revenue, the NGOs say the media, especially the State run media, could be better put to use in the service of development.

Before going further, I would like to quote Gaston Roberge, currently Director of EMRC, Calcutta :

> There is sublime rhetoric about development being the full actualisation of the potential of human persons. As a matter of fact, development is, primarily if not solely, an economic process based on capitalistic development. This is not in the service of those who need, but in the service of the market, now on a global scale. It is amply clear that as an international project, development has little to offer to those most in need of development (whatever the meaning of the term).
>
> —*Gaston Roberge, The Chitrabani Experience*

Communication, and by extension the media, has been coopted into development projects ever since the 1960s. We had the *development media* (from which later grew the term *participatory communication*) to describe a process whereby the poor were seduced, persuaded, cajoled into participating in a particular scheme or project which had been so kindly drawn up for them. Now the NGOs and others came in with alternative development schemes, and then we had *alternative communication* (like street plays) to promote them. With the mainstream media changing its priorities, and the poor realising that the institutions of communication are not really designed to help them, we have reached the end of the road. Or perhaps, the beginning of a new one.

Electronic Media Underutilized

Our experience in the Notre Dame Communication Centre, Patna has pointed to the fact that communication as a tool for development has not been fully understood, and thus, not adequately supported. No doubt, government departments have made many more films since video technology reduced costs, but most viewers tend to take these with a pinch of salt.

In Bihar, activist groups like Kritika and Akhra in Chottanagpur have made telling documentaries about the various issues concerning the Adivasi communities. These films are put across on the local cable networks or shown to groups in villages in order to sensitize them. Such efforts by NGOs have been sporadic and uncoordinated. Somehow, funding agencies are wary of funding video documentation of potentially "explosive" material. NGOs on their part are wary of making hard-hitting films that expose injustice or present the view of the exploited and disadvantaged. It is so easy for vested interests in league with the exploiters to turn the tables on the NGO. A local competent authority can write an official note declaring the film or the NGO to be the cause of community tensions or inciting violence. A single black mark on the NGO's record may mean the denial of its quota of foreign funding.

Communication is a two-way process. It contributes towards development by sending information back and forth between those who plan projects and the beneficiaries of these projects. The media creates an atmosphere of understanding and rapport. In reality, this is not how the system is working. Power relations act as a barrier to information flow.

This is where the "alternative" media steps in. Those working for change must use communication tools to empower people so that they can actively intervene in altering their own life circumstances.

The alternative media addresses itself to the problems, aspirations, and cultural expressions of a specific community. It is necessarily the mirror of that group or community. The images are the images from the group. The voices are the voices of the people.

Women's Feature Service (WFS) in New Delhi is an international feature service. Their studio to prepare programmes for radio broadcast was inaugurated last year. WFS takes the microphone to the city streets, homes, and slums. It presents views and analysis of women in their societies and their perception of local, national and international development.

WFS believes that the rural poor, particularly women, are a vast forgotten radio market. By enlisting their direct help in programming and production, they can become contributors rather than passive listeners. Rural women could easily be trained to use a field recorder. They would be more successful in asking the right questions and getting good responses from rural residents. WFS is campaigning for the reservation of a slot on FM stations for "issue based" radio programmes. Its programmes for AIR and international radio stations have drawn attention.

The Print Media

Recently there has been a spurt in special interest magazines in the country. These magazines, primarily English language ones address special interest groups like teenagers, parents, retired folk, automobile lovers, amateur gardeners, etc. The role of the alternative print media lies in actually bringing together and defining a community, addressing its fears, concerns and issues.

Characteristics of Community Media

The guiding philosophy of community media should be to serve the interests and aspirations of the community. The people should be reached where they are. The intention is to promote human development consciously—at whatever level of educational development, interest or understanding the community is currently at—so that people may learn to diagnose their own problems and clarify their objectives.

Community media must have a well defined purpose. What is to be achieved must be known in specific terms. Everything must be put together so that the people accumulate and integrate knowledge that they can use to make decisions.

The community media person is ideally a member of the community he lives in. He speaks the language of the community, feels and understands its problems, and is able to articulate these feelings, problems and aspirations.

The audience must feel they are an important part of the whole process. In many cases, people know better than planners what is best for themselves. What works for them and what does not. Felix Librero, Associate Professor, Institute of Development Communication (Philippines) in an article on Community Radio says, "Participation gives people a sense of belonging; of purpose; of importance; of achievement. This makes them dynamic partners in the development process."

Community media must be research based, service oriented; and should have built in monitoring systems that helps the media person to automatically monitor and evaluate his (her) performance.

An Evolving Concept

The concept of alternative or community media : print, radio, television is difficult to define. It is an evolving concept. In Bihar, with its diverse layers of language, caste, tribe. . . community media is still a startlingly new concept, largely untested.

Training programmes and courses to enable various groups—women, children, economically or socially disadvantaged—to understand the media and put it to use do exist within the state, but these programmes are few. Such programmes must necessarily be subsidized in order to be brought within the reach of the target groups.

For example, Skills for Progress, a Bangalore based funding agency, regularly funds a television production-cum-still photography course for tribal boys in Bihar and the North East. Some of these trainees have found employment in the mainstream media. At least two of them have opted to work among their own communities in the forests of Chottanagpur, documenting the lives of their people. Such support is rare, however, because agencies would rather fund a tailoring or knitting programme rather than a course which would put the camera or microphone into the hands of rural women.

On the other hand, the opening up of the airwaves presents a unique opportunity for the production and dissemination of issue based programming, which can involve the participation of local communities.

Existing cable networks could be used to broadcast locally made programmes on their "video" channel. The experiment of having local politicians discuss issues on a Patna based cable network was conducted. Efforts to further extend the programme to include production of local talk shows fell through due to lack of advertisement revenue. The idea, mooted three years ago, was a bit early for its time. Today, with the changing broadcast scenario, local issue based programmes could provide an alternative to the mindless march of movie based fare currently being offered on the tube.

There already exists in Bihar professional recording studios that make vernacular programmes for the Hindi services of Radio Manilla and Radio Veritas. With the FM band poised to take off soon, the possibilities in this field are wide open.

The Taru Mitra, a student organisation has recently started a bilingual environmental magazine aimed at school students in Bihar. This magazine seeks to take up various environmental issues and deal with them on the students' terms. Computers and Desk Top Publishing can make small community newsletters a viable means of communication.

Advertising need not be a bad word. Alternative media, with the help of community spirited advertisers and strong community support can certainly be financially viable. As more public service organisations and NGOs come to understand the concept and uses of community media as a tool for sensitization, research, and community building, funding agencies will ultimately cooperate. The possibilities are numerous. The challenge tough but not insurmountable. The age of community media is about to dawn in this land. It is time to wake up and be about and doing!

10

MARKET FORCES AND EDUCATIONAL TELEVISION
Meeting the Pro-Social Challenge

—K. P. MADHU AND VIJAYLUXMI BOSE

The effect that television has had on our society is evident everywhere—in the jungle of antennae which dot the skyline of the major metros and even small towns, the avid discussions about serials and soap operas in the home and even in the workplace. The snatches of jingles that street children sing and the deserted playgrounds are testimony to the fact that children are watching television rather than playing outdoors.

Popular magazines and weekend newspapers also decry the negative effects of this medium. It is now almost universally recognized that television is a medium that cannot be wholly devoted to entertainment. So what do we mean when we say that 'television needs to fulfil its social responsibilities'?

Do we mean that advertisements should be taken off the air? Are we demanding a Public Service Broadcasting System? Are we saying that television should be used as a training and educational tool?

It is high time that such platitudes be transformed into action and the potential of television as an educational medium be explored in its broadest and fullest sense. After all, the advent of satellite television in this country coincided with one of the most innovative experiments in educational broadcasting—the SITE experiment. But at that time, the market was not developed as it is today.

What do we mean by the market?

The market for satellites and transponders,
the market for production equipment,
the market for software,
the market for trained manpower, and
the market for selling and buying time—the time that the viewers give so freely. This time is sold to all other markets, from soap and toothpaste to salt and other tidbits.

We are interested in the way TV has turned commercial and for this we need to understand only the last few markets. The scope of this chapter does not cover the first two market places and is restricted to the other market forces.

Our thesis is that Edutainment—whether it is in the form of educational programmes which are entertaining as well, or entertainment programmes which have a message to impart—is perhaps an alternative to the intervention of market forces which have commercialized the media and are cause for concern among large sections of the populace.

This concern for what is broadcast on television has been written about in newspapers and magazines. The findings of a study conducted jointly by the Media Advocacy Group and the Mass Communication Research Centre (MCRC), Jamia Millia Islamia in New Delhi in 1995 are relevant here.

A cross-section of high, middle and low-income groups was interviewed across the metropolis with the objective of finding out their reactions to the film-based songs which appeared on television regularly. Across the sample, especially women, there was a strong feeling that this was not entertainment meant for the whole family. Some men and women felt that these songs could be viewed very late in the evening (i.e. after the children had gone to bed). The situation is succinctly summed by Sevanti Ninan, the well-known columnist, ". . . . most viewers would want the bump and the grind taken off the peak viewing hours, regardless of whether the advertisers want this or not".

Most of the viewers were able to repeat popular advertisement jingles which appeared in between programmes on television, some even said that ads did influence their buying behaviour. This lends supports the finding that as long as advertisements continue to appear on television, it will fuel consumerism to some extent. Incidentally, the responses were identical for Doordarshan and cable television.

Student projects carried out by the MCRC during the 1995-96 (even though they have very restricted samples) also indicated that children who watch cable television spend less time reading, in outdoor sports and socialize less than those children who do not watch cable television to that extent.

However, some middle and upper income group parents and students do feel that television viewing in general has added to their knowledge. This feeling was reiterated by Bhabani Sengupta in his article published in the *Gentleman* magazine in 1996. Both these research findings (disparate as they may seem), establish the need for some kind of programming which is both entertaining and does lead to some knowledge gain.

The Experiments

There have been some efforts to broad base education through the Countrywide Classroom telecast; the regional telecasts for school education have also been going on for some time; the Indira Gandhi National Open University through its Training and Development Communication Channel is trying to reach skills and knowledge out to a maximum number of people in far-flung areas of the country, using teleconferencing as a tool... But while it is universally acknowledged that satellite television as a medium is capable of delivering education for all to remote and inaccessible areas—the crunch comes when one actually looks into the software necessary for such programming and the problems production of such software.

The Issues : Need for Research in Programming

There can be no doubt that there is tremendous 'information hunger' among certain sections of the population, especially women, adolescents and young adults for example. Studies conducted over the last two years on HIV/AIDS awareness among college-going (and non-student) youth in five states of India, showed that not only was information on AIDS which was broadcast over radio and television inadequate, but the nature of the messages was such that it had led to a great deal of confusion on part of the youngsters. Across all income groups, focus group discussions indicated a tremendous fear of HIV/AIDS, there was also confusion between AIDS and other life-threatening diseases and a tremendous need to know more about this pandemic.

The reason for this is clear. Just as one campaign (let alone a single programme) does not bring about an attitude shift among the audience, there are some intervening processes which occur between formative research (prior to production), programme production and the monitoring of effects. When these processes occur not once but repeatedly and the entire loop is completed, only then one can see any discernible signs of attitude-shift. Any short-cuts lead to the confusion and distortion described so graphically by Hamelink.

It is crucial that comprehension of these programmes is monitored, that existing knowledge-levels of the audience are assessed prior to the programmes being made, if these fears and myths about AIDS are to be allayed to some extent.

Research by Yadava (1988) on Indian families responses to television reveals that physical placement of a television set within the home is crucial to family viewing. According to Nass *et al.* (1996) television in a sense is a place where events happen, and the closer one is to television, the closer one is to the forefront of events. Similarly, when respondents are asked about programme preferences and formats for HIV/AIDS, sex and sexuality have stressed that programmes should be made for family viewing.

Some of these results have changed the programmes being made and telecast about HIV/AIDS, thanks to the efforts of some NGOs. But it serves to establish a fundamental truth about the effects of television : the nature and design of the programmes which are telecast is important if the message has to be faithfully delivered.

Research on the relevance of the programme to target audiences is likewise important. While it is also universally known that audience memory is transient, there are enough examples from the entertainment industry (e.g. *Humlog*), entertainment and education (e.g. *Chowraha* or the '*Meena*' series on the girl child), the lyrical '*Mile Sur Hamara*' from LSSP and the most recent series of spots from the National Literacy Mission which most people seem to remember.

The Issues : Limitations of Television

Another fact that the above-mentioned studies highlighted was the importance of counselling and interpersonal communication. As a follow-up to these studies, the MCRC with an international NGO called the NAZ Foundation (India) Trust, conducted experimental peer-counselling sessions, using the same sample used in the studies as a control group. It was found that the sample group learnt much faster, was able to utilize what was taught during the counselling sessions and were prime peer counsellors because they had been able to discuss their fears about HIV/AIDS in earlier Focus Group Discussions with the MCRC research team, while they were conducting their study.

Cees Hamelink in his book *Trends in World Communication* (Southbound, 1994) has stated "Today's institutions and processes of world communication have a disempowering effect . . . The withholding and distorting of information obstructs people's independent formation of opinion and undermines peoples capacity to control decisions that affect their daily lives". This is linked to the stereotypical way in which women and minorities are portrayed in television programmes.

What was written in the late 1980s on the role of television in society stands true of Indian television today. Gerbner *et al.* (1986) have called television a centralized system of storytelling, which is the part of the daily lives of many, many people. "Its drama, commercials, news and other programmes bring a relatively coherent world of common images and messages into every home".

But now, faced with a multi-channel situation, a plethora of entertainment to choose from, why should the average viewer, switch on to an educational programme. What is the motivation for that person to do so?

It is not only the medium, nor only the message but the social marketing of messages, formative, process impact research which should form the basis for edutainment. These are some issues to consider as approaches to edutainment based pro-social programming, which we feel, is an alternative to the commercial onslaught on the media.

In another article on 'Using Television to Best Advantage', Johnston and Ettema (1986) have also made some observations which are relevant to the role television has to play in Indian society if it is to fulfil its pro-social obligations and provide a challenge to market forces. "The goal of producers of most commercial shows that come to be called pro-social is to entertain and thereby attract as large an audience as possible . . . Among non-commercial and educational producers, entertainment may also be a goal because holding an audience is *sine qua non* for other socialization goals".

The Issues : Software

It is impossible to be prescriptive about edutainment—there are far too many weak links in the chain, who will produce the programmes? Why should commercial producers suddenly start getting interested in edutainment? (asking them to include a social message within every programme is definitely not the answer!) Why should industries and the corporate sector suddenly start sponsoring such programmes?

These questions have to be tackled as a single problem because they are related to each other. Talent and training would have to meet with money and motivation to solve these problems.

The reason for the persistence of these problems is partly due to the fact that not enough empirical evidence exists to indicate what it is that audiences truly want and whether such programmes are viable commercially or not.

The other is motivation—education programme production (as it stands today) is just not as paying as entertainment. The returns are not so quick and the glitz and glamour is missing.

If we can provide enough evidence to show that viewership, television ratings, rates of spot-buys/air-time and effectiveness of various television channels in changing consumer preferences, etc. have no rational relationship in reality, but have value only in discourse and arguments, or, if we can motivate young talented software professionals to forsake a career in advertising and get on with educational programming, then, and only then, can we solve the basic issues facing us.

In an article on Indian Software Policies, Stephen McDowell (1995) has said that the information revolution in India has been shaped by informatics, software production and by phenomenal growth of commercially funded and entertainment-oriented satellite services, cable television networks, private radio broadcasting and sales and rentals of audio-visual recordings. "It remains to be seen whether India's policy record in promoting a software industry as a niche within the global information economy can translate into information and communication services that better serve broader demands and needs within India".

What are these needs? First and foremost education has to be seen in a wider and more applied context; secondly it has to be related to the daily lives of the people.

Distance education formats are changing from the virtual classroom situation, to mass-based training programmes, which are tailor-made for certain user groups be they panchayat representatives, primary school teachers or management trainees. In view of the market forces within the changed economic scenario, effective and efficient service delivery systems are essential. Using satellites for such initiatives cannot only bring down the running costs of the training programme (apart from the initial cost of installing a VSAT) but can reach out quality education and training to large numbers of people, such as teachers, rural development and health functionaries, women and child development facilitators—to name a few especially those located in remote areas.

In one of his lectures, Kiran Karnik (1996) has spoken about decentralization of the media in view of the near-impossibility of imposing controls on information flows, especially in the age of miniaturization. Lower costs of reception and transmission will, he feels, result in better information flows both in terms of quantum and efficiency (The Vikram Sarabhai Memorial Lecture August, 1996). In this context, one can think of mass-based education in the wider sense of the term i.e. usable knowledge, information for skills-development and empowerment. This is also an area where eventually market forces will take over—making these centres of information self-sustaining, just as the STD-ISD-PCO venture is today. Karnik very correctly predicts the development of the 'infoentrepreneurs'.

The Bottomline

In the past there have been two lobbies vying intensely for attention—one that argues that commercial sponsoring be done away with and the other which holds fast to the idea that there can be parallel streams of programming, if enough planning is undertaken.

In a market-driven economy the force of finances would dictate terms. So, a private television channel without commercial sponsorship would be a tall order in these days. But the state-run channels would have support infortainment and edutainment till the communication technologies are fully matured and cross fertilizations take place.

A Glimpse into 2000 A. D.

Communication research and production of programmes for educational television must take into account the changing communication scenarios. Hamelink (1994) has aptly described the current trend as a 'Trend Towards Consolidation'—"as all signals, whether they carry sound, data, or pictures, converge into the digital format, they become, however, different in substance, identical in the technical sense. As a result, telecommunication and broadcasting integrate . . .". Recent research indicates that responses to television content (i.e. programmes) may be changed when television sets are assigned particular roles.

There is also very little difference in peoples' responses to computers when compared to their responses to television. Moreover, social responses to communication technologies are fundamental and such technologies have the ability to easily elicit social responses. This finding (Clifford Nass *et al*., 1996) should play a key role for communication designers in new communication technologies and interfaces.

Internet is an example of communication which is devoid of 'the shackles of linearity'. The Internet plays with the Source-Message-Channel-Receiver features of traditional mass communication models which would give rise to new configurations of messaging. Communication on the Internet will be redefined in terms of the reader-audience, where the Internet member-receiver shoulders a lot more responsibility since the Internet offers a vast range of communication opportunities especially interactivity (Rafaeli, *Journal of Communication*, Winter, 1996).

In India, this medium is being used by the commercial sector, the medical profession, academics, etc. but needs to have many more users from all sectors of the population, especially those in rural areas. The Ninth Plan envisages computers for all village panchayats; Internet facilities for farmers, databases in local languages; these technologies do mean some amount of computer penetration in remote areas.

However, preceding the introduction of a new technology or even an innovative use of existing technology means that certain innovative research techniques are necessary. Pro-social television is an active enterprise; the goal of sustainability of any communication activity must always be kept as an achievable objective.

This kind of communication environment presents two challenges—one of culturally sensitive software, and the other in innovative research skills and techniques. If we need intelligent and creative programming which takes up the technological tools available in the market to add value to our huge population, there has to be a concurrent commitment from different layers of our community.

The Agenda

In today's environment, the market forces have an edge, since they have the resources to command the best skills. But efforts like the Countrywide Classroom, the Pij transmission and Sewa video have shown that video can be used creatively and constructively, both in the broadcast and the narrow cast mode.

What emerges from the above discussion is that there must be some amount of agenda-setting by educational media, the audience for such programmes must be cultivated and the environment built up in such a way that it presents a viable alternative to the entertainment industry.

Recently some voices have been raised on the need for a national media policy, and the need to have public service broadcasting. Unless we have a policy which allows and encourages a plurality of voices the cultural and linguistic diversity in the country cannot be sustained.

REFERENCES

Bose, Vijayluxmi and Archana R. Singh (1994). AIDS awareness among young adults in Madras, MCRC and AIDSCAP-FHI, Unpublished.

Bose, Vijayluxmi *et al.* (1994). AIDS awareness among college students in four states of India. MCRC-UTA study. Unpublished.

Gerbner, George, Larry Gross *et al.* (1986). Living with television : The dynamics of the cultivation process. In : *Perspectives on Media Effects*, Jennings Bryant and Dolf Zillman (eds). Lawrence Erlbaum Associates.

Johnston, Jerome and James Ettema (1986). Using television for best advantage. In : *Perspectives on Media Effects*, Jennings Bryant and Dolf Zillman (eds). Lawrence Erlbaum Associates.

Karnik, Kiran (1996). The Vikram Sarabhai Memorial Lecture. The Vikram Sarabhai Foundation.

McDowell, Stephen (1995). The decline of the license Raj : Indian software export policies. *Journal of Communication.*

Mody, Bella (1995). State consolidation through liberalization of telecommunications services in India. *Journal of Communication.*

Morris Merrill and Christine Ogan (1996). The Internet as mass medium-Indiana University. *Journal of Communication.*

Nass, Clifford *et al.* (1996). Technology and roles : A tale of two TVs. *Journal of Communication.*

Nazki, Hilal Ahmed (1995-96). A study on the impact of cable television on school children. MCRC-JMI, student thesis, Unpublished.

Ninan, Sevanti (1994). DD's porno shows. *The Hindu*, 8 May 1994.

Newhagen, John E. and Sheizal (1996). Internet—A dialogue. *Journal of Communication.*

Hamelink Cees (1994). Trends in world communication (Southbound, 1994).

Vohra, Sonia. Television, sex and teenagers. MCRC-JMI, student thesis, Unpublished.

Yadava, J. S. (1988). In the midst of diversity : Television in urban Indian homes. In : *World Families Watch Television.* Sage Publications.

11

EDITORIAL LEADERSHIP IN NEWSPAPERS

Decay of an Institution

—GOPAL MISRA

It is not an effort to plead for the continuance of editorial supremacy in a newspaper establishment, but the issue is whether it is necessary to keep old values regarding the role of the editor, or we accept the influence of market forces reducing a newspaper editor as one of the departmental heads such as those looking after the advertisement or circulation sections of a publication house. In this context, it is necessary that the growth of newspapers as the fourth most important institution of the state after executive, legislature and judiciary has to be analyzed. It has emerged as a continuous forum in a democratic society, where the editor's supremacy is considered necessary as an impartial umpire to act as the guardian of free exchange of views and uninterrupted flow of information.

As the process of modernization is also related to the capacity of a society to absorb new ideas, we must realize whether in recent years Indian society has kept its strength to successfully picked up new ideas in every field or it has now lost its capacity to join the new emerging economies of the world on the eve of the new century. It is true that during the past 150 years or so, Indians have shown rare capacity of a backward society to pick up new ideas, whether it was the question of setting up modern democratic institutions or new ideas for faster socio-economic developments. This success is also reflected in the country's efforts to educate itself in the high-tech areas. The founders of this modern Indian state had a very clear conception of the country's socio-economic conditions and the factors, which were responsible for its failure to save itself during the colonial era of nineteenth century. Apart from the caste barriers, it was also accepted that women must have equal role in modern India. The idea of gender equality was a part of our freedom movement and it was realized that for a rapid socio-economic transformation, the modern Indian state should accept a secular, democratic society having sound parliamentary system of government. But the growing opposition to social causes must make us aware of the new challenges being faced by the Indian society. And the role of media has to be re-stressed in this new environment.

During the freedom struggle, these ideas were a part of the country's main political agenda, which also accepted newspapers as a vanguard of people's rights. On these issues, newspapers were considered as a continuous campaigners and its editors were also considered social reformers, who as an impartial and neutral authority were expected to keep a close vigil on the socio-economic and political trends in the country.

It is time to assess that how far the journalists and newspapers have succeeded in this task of nation building. Admittedly, the newspapers and its editors have not been able to assert on these issues, as their predecessors could do before independence. During the half-a-century of our existence as an independent country, we are witnessing certain aberrations, as we have started compromising on the basic ideology which is the basis of our democratic society. A Hindi daily published by a national group from New Delhi did not take stand against the "burning of a woman on husband's pyre". Similarly, on the issue giving reservations to women in state legislatures and Parliament, the language newspapers, which have much more readership than the English dailies have not made it a burning issue of the day. It is learnt that the owner-editors of the language newspapers are not supporting these social causes. The journalists working in these institutions have little voice. If there is a resistance to the Constitutional Bill which will give 33 per cent share to women in the country's Parliament and state legislatures, there is also a deliberate effort by the powerful sections of the society opposed to social reforms, which ultimately compromises the concept of free press and its legitimate role in a democracy.

It may appear that the two issues are separate and cannot be related to each other. But an in-depth analysis will explain that there is a deliberate attempt to scuttle the process of modernization in the country. Sometimes, market forces are being blamed for the institutional decay in various sectors of our society, but seldom it is realized that the modern democracy is the result of the market forces. The struggle for democratic institutions has always been due to the inability of the then existing feudal systems to respond to the changing socio-economic scenario of the nineteenth century. The old state structure had collapsed following the growth of technology and trade, which made people less dependent upon the state. But the old order was replaced by modern institutions, and as the result of these changes, which helped the newspapers to emerge as a continuous forum for information, discussion and debates, a vital institution of a democracy.

It was a part of the political transformation of the feudal era to a democratic polity irrespective of its various forms. While in the feudal era, the powers of the state were vested in an individual, but gradually the state powers were divided into three distinctive parts—executive, legislature and judiciary. And in eliminating the decadent feudal era, newspapers' pioneer role has been recognized and a modern democracy cannot be visualised without its powerful newspapers.

The evolution of free press was first witnessed in England, which was also accompanied by the emergence of the institution of editors. India under the British rule was also influenced by these democratic institutions and we too have a band of eminent editors who helped in the growth of independent journalism in the country. Those who helped in establishing the free press in India, include Ambica Prasad Vajpeyi, who is still remembered as father of modern Hindi journalism, and Sadanand and Rama Rao who helped in setting up modern English language newspapers such as Free Press Journal and National Herald, respectively, which were devoted to the cause of India's independence. These newspapers, while opposing the continuance of the British Raj in India were equally concerned towards the socio-economic uplift of the society. The editors and other journalists always believed that India's problem lies in its social backwardness, which ultimately led to its subjugation by foreign powers.

In the post-independence era, the problem of the functioning of free press started following acquisition of the British-owned newspapers by Indian capitalists. These newspapers such as *Times of India* and *Statesman* having vast resources at their disposal overshadowed the nationalist press. Under the new Indian ownership, these papers became the country's main-stream dailies. Thus, the influence of the nationalist press, which had earned respect during the freedom struggle, waned in the past three decades or so. The Anglo-Indian press now under the Indian owners changed their policy from being a supporter of the British Raj, they started espousing the cause of the business classes. Even the concept of freedom of press to disseminate information was quietly changed in favour of projecting the views favouring the business interests of the newspaper owners.

These subtle changes in the country's media scene, which started in early fifties has now totally influenced the concept of freedom of expression—which is now more devoted to selling new electronic gadgets or consumer durables than discussing the problems related to common people living in abject poverty.

During the initial years, these Indian owners allowed their editors to retain some of the old British tradition of giving respect to the editors. But the second generation of these owners, educated in English medium schools, have become more assertive as newspaper owners. Some of them even have created the post of managing editor to have a direct control over the newspapers, and thus the professional editor has been totally sidelined and relegated from its pre-eminent position. There is nothing wrong, if the owners of a publications exercise control over the editorial, but the issue is larger, if a newspaper has to act as a forum of a vibrant democracy, it must have an editorial leadership committed to the socio-economic uplift of the society. But if a newspaper has to cater only to the needs of a business house, it will lose its value as a permanent forum for discussion and debate. It will become only a house journal of a business establishment.

The issue of editorial supremacy has to be examined from this perspective and it should not be confused by the so-called pressures being mounted by the market forces on the media and newspapers. The fact is the concept of free press is a part of a democratic system, which successfully has ousted the feudal system, because the old ruling elite could not measure up to the new socio-economic needs of the society. Now the challenge before the society is how to take entire society a beneficiary of the new technologies and the economic growth, but newspapers have yet to respond the situation. In this context, it is necessary that we should also examine the impact of the new pressures on newspapers. A close scrutiny of country's major newspapers reveals that the major dailies have distanced themselves from the people's issues and are giving more space to fashion, beauty contests, and there appears to be a deliberate effort on the part of these publications to ignore the issues yearning for an immediate media attention. Admittedly, there has to be some interesting items to keep the readership interests, but the expansion of newspapers do not reflect that they have gained the readership enjoyed by their counterparts in the developed world.

The analysis will remain inconclusive, if some attention is not paid to the negative role of the journalists in undermining their own institutions. If we closely examine the trend of the past two decades or so, the newspapers have lost much of their credibility because there was no serious effort to train the new generation to realize the sensitive role a newspaper plays in a society. The glamour pages on fashions and films are like to keep the readership interests in the newspaper. The shifting of focus of newspapers from hard news to these soft areas has deliberately done by journalists themselves. Some of them even do not hesitate to undertake the job of public relationing to please their employers. All this is being done in name of economic liberalization.

It is also necessary to examine the economic gains of journalists in this new dispensation. Their salaries have gone up, and they are equally paid as any other executive. But this executive lifestyle has undermined the journalist's basic role as a social reformer and a neutral umpire of a forum for free flow of information. The decay of the institution of newspapers and their editors as the continuous forum of a vibrant democracy should be examined and analyzed in this context. If they want to rehabilitate themselves in their old role, they must also forget about the executive lifestyle and devote themselves to their basic role of a journalist, the future of newspapers so far appears to be bleak as a vehicle of social change, if the current trend of newspapers' contents are not revised. They may reduce themselves as information sheets without having social commitments.

12

ALTERNATIVE MEDIA INSTITUTIONS

—MELISSA BUTCHER

In almost every paper we have heard at this colloquium, the words "degrading our culture" have appeared. I would like to ask what is it you are trying to preserve. Whose culture? Brahmanic, Dalit, Muslim, Buddhist, Women's culture, tribal culture, northern, southern? What exactly is the basic value system of India? How is it changing and what is it changing into? Instead of addressing these questions, there is a tendency to target the media, television in particular, as the sole carrier of a culturally alien lifestyle market-driven consumerism, that is "invading" our country and denigrating our way of life. Television's position as a constant in our homes to which our children seem to be mesmerised adds to the concern. With the plethora of channels now available, television has become fast, flashy and visually represents all that is modern, that is, the much maligned 'Western'.

But television is not an autonomous, self-perpetuating organism. So, we cannot just wring our hands and solely blame the media for cultural change, for "corrupting the minds of our youth", without examining the wider social and economic policies prevalent in India today. As a technological conduit I would agree that television has changed the way images are processed. Audiences can at times perceive a sense of authority and legitimisation to new limit images attached to behavioural codes, because they have come to them via the television. Yet while the imagery and messages advocates a particular direction of development, television does not itself generate that direction. That comes from other sources which must also be addressed. Those that have advocated media as the denigrator of culture have at times been the same voices which continue to support the current liberalisation policies which allow that process to occur. The media becomes their scapegoat. Therefore, rather than focusing on television *per se*, let's look at the creation of market forces. Who benefits? It is not just multinational or western companies, but Indian channels, Indian advertisers, Indian business enterprises, Indian government policies are also involved.

The liberalisation of economy in India equates a governing by the market. Television simply operates within the same laissez-faire principles. As much spectacle, entertainment, sport, soap opera, as the public, in its role as arbitrator of the market, will bear. The commercialisation of the media reflects market forces in its offering of 'freedom of choice'. Certainly there is more choice for the consumer now in terms of the number of channels. But we could agree with writer Ien Ang who says that we are in fact *condemned* to a freedom of choice. As I channel-surf through the 30-odd stations available in Delhi, there appears very little choice in terms of content. We would probably all agree that the choice for consumers is not always edifying media product, and that there is a problem with the associated commercialisation and consumerism that must go with it to pay for the special effects. Nor is the consumer given any choice in the programming, in the scheduling, or the structuring of media. The consumer has no choice as to the direction of change in India, in its choice of economic development, or even a choice in representation of identity in television texts.

Seen from a more holistic view, the particular problem becomes not so much market forces *per se*, which are only an aspect of a broader dimension of national change, but with the nature of change itself. A national dichotomy is emerging between that labelled as 'tradition' and that as 'modern'. Under these rubrics come a number of normative judgements : one is good, the other is bad; one is 'old fashioned', the other is 'rational' and 'efficient'. Market forces are 'modern'. What are these market forces? They are an ideology, a part of the knowledge system derived from a particular cultural and geographical nexus. They are not inevitable but part of an historical process. Nor are they in any sense autonomous. They are a conglomeration of individual and institutional thought and action; a dialectic between consumer and producer.

Modernity, and market forces in particular, have become synonymous with "the West". To maintain an indigenous identity, tradition has inevitably become synonymous with local cultural values and demarcated as something that needs to be preserved to protect us from 'the West'. This prophylactic culture has been deconstructed, recomposed, and regurgitated, particularly through visual imagery. It can become itself stylised for the consumption of television audiences, of which the recent 'showcasing' of Indian culture during the Miss World pageant is a fine example. To attempt to ossify a culture through mediated images in a traditional exhibition would seem as harmful as the mediation of the current frenetic pace of change.

When we speak of cultural impact of the media it is not possible any longer, with the body of research that has accumulated over the years, to speak of a monolithic imposition of culture through television, like a hypodermic needle straight from advertiser to viewer. The importance of the local response, the individual reading through a complex haze of local cultural conditioning and influences, moves us away from the idea of 'the masses'. The masses do not behave or respond with one voice. India is a multitude of voices. Factors involved in determining how audiences will interpret programme content, what they accept and reject, includes parents, school, friends, local culture and rituals, local definitions of what is right and wrong. Interpersonal communication and socialisation processes seem crucial in the understanding of television imagery. The move to Hindisation of foreign channels, STAR Plus' recent rescheduling, is perhaps an indication of the pressure of the local reading on market forces. Yet again, this can be interpreted as the co-option of this local reading, the *localisation of international products*, converting them to local tastes and in so doing further expanding the commercial market.

Ultimately, however, commercial television is not going to depart from India's screens. Whether we like it or not they do provide popular programming and as long as there is money to be made they will stay. If we wish to take action against the current trend in commercialisation of programming, foreign content, etc., we must also look at the national and global scene. Are we in fact asking for another model of development, or merely for television to broadcast programming considered more 'cultural' by a particular segment of Indian society.

It would seem more effective at this time, particularly as the government proposes new Broadcasting legislation this winter, to look at different ways the media can provide an alternative not just to current programming trends, but also to counter market forces and in so doing provide a role for itself in an alternative development agenda.

As media professionals, researchers, and consumers can we not ensure that alternatives are provided that address in particular questions of representation and participation of the audience. The creation of a new space, space for Public Service Broadcasting, space for Community Media. Should we not be ensuring adequate and assured funding for such services, made possible through various methods : properly regulated government allocations, licensing of television sets, a tax on advertising revenues, subsidies to software houses to ensure the production of educational and development packages. Digitisation of satellite transponders means more channels but also niche marketing, making smaller audiences more attractive to advertisers which will also perhaps allow more specialised programming to be made. Should we not be attempting to make stronger images than those produced by the benefactors of the current development model. And should we not be attempting to make this a world project, as the grief we feel at the intangible sense of loss created by 'modern' change is not contained within India alone, but is felt in communities globally.

Alternative Media Institutions

While it is to other countries we look to find the source of this grief, it is also to them that we could look to see examples of how alternative media institutions and image forms can be created and sustained. The Public Broadcasting Services of the United States, Australia, Canada and Britain have merits which could be adjusted to the Indian context. The Special Broadcasting Service of Australia, with particular niche language programming still broadcasts arguably the best current affairs and documentary programming in that country with minimal sponsorship and government funding. The American feminist magazine, Ms, does not take advertising but survives on subscription alone. Non-profit community radio with active local participation has proven itself to be very successful in Africa, and Latin America in terms of development communication. Radio Sagarmatha in Nepal is a fine example of a community station that, while it must still wait for government permission to begin broadcasting, has established its studio in Kathmandu and trained programme makers. Another example from Nepal is a local cable operator in the rural North who began to make local programmes as well as broadcast STAR network. I am told that on weekends, when these local programmes are aired, they have become so popular that there are very few people in the street. Doordarshan already has infrastructure for effective local broadcasting, over 700 low powered transmitters which, with funding, could be transformed into local production units. An emphasis on the local could help to counter the rural/urban divide in India if it allows for more input to the centre from the periphery. Or if you prefer, from the bottom up, a process of cultural subversion perhaps, where public advocacy is encouraged and media monologue is replaced by dialogue.

13

EMERGING MARKET FORCES AND RESPONSIBILITY OF MEDIA

—RADHE SHYAM SHARMA

We are passing through a period of "Information Explosion". This is the age of information. The electronic media, particularly satellite channels have completely changed the media scenario. All informations have now been reaching in the homes, This has not only changed the psychology of people but also changed their approach and life style in offices as well as in homes. With the revolution in communication technology, any information can reach in every part of the world within no time. The information explosion has particularly affected the minds of the young generation.

The information revolution has also changed the thinking process throughout the world. The whole approach and emphasis has taken altogether a new turn. During eighties and nineties, economic factors had displaced military power as the prime arbiter. The best examples of the results of this development are the ascendancy of Japan and Germany, in the world power structure. In fact once Germany's currency saved Dollar in the world market. The economic strength of then West Germany was responsible mainly for re-unification of both Germanys. The primacy of economic factor also played a major part in the dissolution of the Soviet Empire. The people inside the iron curtain came to know the realities of the world. The dictatorship of the proletariat could not resist its people from demanding more freedom and fulfilment of needs.

The population, land mass and natural resources are now no more big power potential. These are the old concepts. In the modern world, technology quality has greater and bigger role than even Industrial Revolution. The information revolution and communication technology is now playing a bigger role.

On international level, the trend began to set to suit the industrially advanced countries and legitimised the conquest of empires. This in turn enabled these countries, many of which lacked natural resources to augment their shortfalls from their empire. The heavier dependence on technology, naturally led to economic attributes taking the second place gradually without challenging as yet the emerging primacy of military attributes. An example of this apparent waning of the importance of population and land mass in the power equation was transformation of Britain that lacked these basic attributes into Great Britain.

With the advent of Information Technology Revolution the world is fashioning itself into a knowledge-based power structure.

One important fact is that Information Revolution has helped in globalisation. People today know more about the world today than few decades back. That is why there is also a talk of cultural invasion. However, it is difficult to remain aloof in present world and different cultures will have their impact on others. There are attempts to keep different communities and their cultural identities intact by emotional appeal or by fanatism. Even then it is difficult to resist the impact of other cultures or thoughts because of information explosion. The Iron Curtain of Soviet Union could not resist the pressure of people to have freedom of expression and free economy. Information revolution in fact prepared ground for it.

When Mr. Rupert Murdock arrived in Japan in June 1996, the Media Executives there, were puzzled. His visit was termed as unexpected invasion of foreign capital and its advance into their turf. Murdock bought 21 per cent of prestigious Asahi T.V. The Japanese Prime Minister Ryutaro Hashimoto then commented that Mr. Murdock's entry into Japan was natural in line with a global trend. Such trend is visible throughout the world today and it is bound to affect social, national and individual life styles as well as thinking process.

The Information Explosion has changed the look, content and presentation of newspapers. The TV has helped people in making their opinion after seeing events on the screen. This has affected their thinking process and approach towards life. TV has today become a powerful medium of communication. Thus, its role has become very important. The information explosion has brought more openness. This has also affected the political and social systems and the market. No government can now keep its people in the dark or in any illusion. People can see the happenings in any corner of the world with the help of electronic media and they can form their own opinion. Due to information explosion all types of controls on the flow of information have become almost impossible. The flow of information has also been responsible for changes in the society. This has also accelerated the pace of technological development and economic progress. The Information Technology Revolution has greater impact on Agricultural and Industrial Revolution. Both the revolutions have affected man's life and living. All the three have also been major civilisation revolutions.

The main function of media, including TV, has been to inform and educate people. The films and TV added the new function of entertainment to it. But there is very thin line between entertainment and proper communication as the market forces have started dominating the media, particularly the TV. As there are large number of satellites and TV channels, they try to attract the advertisers. The manufacturers have found TV to be the most effective media to sell their goods by the help of advertisements and sponsored serials. To make their programmes attractive and popular they attach glamour to it. The overdose of sex and violence in programmes has become the order of the day. This all had its effect on the minds of the younger generation. With arrival of foreign media on large scale, it is said, that there is cultural invasion. This has changed the life style and also food habits of the people. Consumerism and commercialisation have also changed their living habits. It is often alleged that we are drifting away from our own culture and identity. Western culture has been dominating the lifestyle. Thus, sometimes it is felt that people lose respect for their own culture.

The market forces know their target market. They have turned the whole media into a big business. Both newspapers and electronic media have become tools in the hands of market forces who are using them for earning more and more profits. The newspaper field is no more a mission. It has become a profession, rather an industry. Due to revolution in printing, communication and information technology, there is vast change in the newspapers. Now more emphasis is on sale and advertisements. The Institution of Editors is eroding and the management is dominating. The earnings through advertisements decide the policy of the newspapers. Advertisements do more than sell products or services. They also sell story of their times. The advertisements and their styles show country's commercial history, its changing social mores and life styles, its fads and fancies and trends. To increase the circulation newspapers resort to sensationalism and sex in their advertisements. Many periodicals publish naked or half-naked photos of women to attract more readership. Some TV channels sometimes resort to blue films, which includes the publicity of their product. There is more of cheap entertainments than education. The standard of programmes is sometimes very low. They have to see that consumer buys only their product. They have to exist in competitive free market.

The advertisers also adopt same tactics. Sometimes the quantum of advertisements in a serial is so much that it becomes disgusting to see it. With the entry of multinationals and liberalism, the market forces have become stronger. They have been dominating in both the social as well as economic fields. This will give rise to economic exploitation. In our country where large population lives below poverty line, rise in consumerism and domination of market forces will increase disparities. The social tensions will also increase. In the race for profits through advertising, there is always a tendency to compromise with social values. The cut throat competition gives rise to underhand tactics. The market forces always bring pressures on producers to change the programmes to suit their needs. The episodes full of sex, crime and violence are repeated very often. This creates tensions in the society. The vulgarity spoils social atmosphere.

The communication is a means, which can be used both ways. Through this the society gets entertainment and information. The information can be concerning education, agricultural development, social upliftment, national integration, social and human values, national defence, liberation from poverty and backwardness and growth of an individual personality. The same media can be used for selfish interests only to earn money and worldly property at any cost. The market forces have no concern to see that people develop a scientific temper, which is very much needed today, as this is the age of science and technology. If the mind is not trained to use modern means in the interest of humanity then the evil mind can lead to disasters. This is what happening today. Inspite of material progress and information explosion there is no end to conflicts, wars, unrest, exploitation, colonial tendencies and profiteering and lack of justice.

It is the duty of the media to change this trend by using communication and information techniques in a way which can uplift human mind. It is to be seen, that market forces are kept within control and do not go out of control. The economy is for the people and for the society. Society is not for economy. The market forces have to look into the interests of the society. Uncontrolled and cheap advertisements and selling substandard goods through wide publicity is a crime. The media has to decide as to which advertisements are worth carrying and which can damage the social fibre. The national and social interests have to be safeguarded. The history shows that the country became slave when foreign powers captured political power through business. The producer is free to earn profits but money is not everything. The needs of a healthy society and its future have to be kept in mind.

It was possible to run commercial traffic in TV. Commercial traffic meant more business and more rush for advertisements. It also meant millions more users every year and consequently an increase in demands for more goods. This was all due to Internet.

It is good that at some places the TV is being used for imparting education to students. The satellite system has also helped the scheme of distant education. Many channels are engaged in education programmes. This is encouraging. The market forces have to see that media also meets the requirement of the society. There has to be a balance between profit motive and welfare of the society. Market forces are a part of the whole system in the country. They cannot be kept above national interests. The media controlled by the government has also to be disciplined and properly used keeping in view the social values.

Media has to be responsible towards the country. It is also answerable to the society. No doubt it needs money to run itself. The advertisements are the biggest source of income. The market forces control the advertisement field and the government is also an important advertiser. It can create balance in this regard. The psyche of the market forces is to dominate the market and through it, dominate the economy. This cannot be allowed. The situation of free for all, can create economic and political anarchy. The media has to be used for constructive purposes also.

The need of the hour is to see that proper balance is kept between industrial production, consumption, market and sales. The economic development and human values, both have to be kept in mind. The media has a responsibility to create an atmosphere and thinking to keep that balance. Only media can do it. The TV channels and cable operators will have to resist the pressures of market forces. The government media can come to the aid of the saner elements who are running such channels.

14

MEDIA AND MARKET FORCES
Social Responsibility

—RAJESHWAR DYAL

That the private capital and commercial businesses have become key factors in the expansion of new media and information industries is illustrated from the except from Media Development (1994) reproduced below :

> The scramble for the media and information market is reminiscent of the scramble for territory in colonial times. Except that this war is being won and lost in corporate board-rooms, on the stock market, in the financial corridors of the world and finally in the hyper-saturated media environments of our lives.

Media—both print as well Broadcast—are no longer considered public service, these are being increasingly referred to as industries—entertainment industries, cultural products; packaging and presentation are becoming more important than substance—all under the impact of market forces. The world over the buzz words are : "Commodification" and "Commercialisation of media".

The process of liberalisation, underway in the country since 1991, is having a profound impact the way business of media is conducted. Media is becoming more and more technology-driven; the opening up of economy has witnessed not only an unflux of foreign networks beaming into the Indian market, but also many Indian companies got uplinked from various satellites spread across the globe. Many publishing houses are diversifying into television production. All this has resulted in stiff competition forcing Doordarshan to open its door to privatisation.

To savour the flavour of contemporary media scenario, here is an other brief reference from the chapter—Open Markets and the Future of Television—Fiction and fact; GATT, GATS and World Trade Organisation, by David French and Michael Richards :

> Satellite television, with its ownership in the hands of buccaneering capitalists, has then been a crucial factor in this process of change. The earlier parts of this book illustrate this in a variety of ways. But it is crucial to understand that the process of technological convergence has not just been a matter of changing technology but also of the importation into the domain of television of vigorously commercial approaches. If satellites are associated with names such as Ted Turner and Rupert Murdoch, then the business of computing and digital technology resonates as strongly with those of Bill Gates and his younger contemporaries. Crucially, the industries and technologies with which broadcasting is converging have always been led by private capital and have only in aberrant national circumstances been subject to regulation for the public good. In other words, if countries wish to jump on the broadband highway, collectively to ride the Internet and the Worldwide Web, then they have, superficially at least, to speak its language and that is the language of private capital and of the free market.

The sweeping wave of commercialisation has evoked strong concern all around—conscientious citizens, parents, academics, social workers, NGOs, consumer activists are aghast at the marketing on-slaught and its impact on different sections of society.

During the recent past a number of research studies, presentations and articles in newspapers and magazines have focused attention on the impact of advertising on children. It has been pointed out that the alien values being encouraged by the commercial media—pop culture in particular—fuelled by the massive engines of capitalism, with profit, its only God, is geared towards producing consumers not citizens. The worry of the parents is given the surfeit of kitsch and wave of consumerism; what is the food for thought on which the child is being nourished.

In several seminars the case of the little boy, who was killed while trying to bungee-jump in the way shown in the Thums up ad. proves how insensitively a company can act to promote its products. Now, again, the same and is back with a disclaimer, which is so fleeting that it fails to register its impression on the child's mind while the child is being aggressively wooed and targetted as a consumer of the advertised goods. What are the types of TV programmes available for the children? According to the findings of a study, conducted by the Asian Media Information and Communication Centre, Singapore, in India, children's programmes comprise less than one per cent of total programming time taking all channels into account. The study points out that the biggest and most damaging gap in the programming is the absence of relevant and interesting programmes for those in their early teens.

So what do we conclude about television's responsibility towards an important segment of its audience—the children; it is that they are a precious commodity for being used in marketing their products and using them for TV ads; as far as educational and relevant programmes for them are concerned, it is none of our (Doordarshan) business. In short children are seduced by the hard sell of marketing techniques.

The impact of marketing forces on print media is equally damaging. According to prevailing practice, the news has to be shaped to fit the new format, determined by the computer screen, even if reports are cut in mid-paragraph. Packaging is becoming more important than content. This has facilitated the increase of owner-editors. The desire to maximise revenue has overcome professional values. Yet it is the Editor who figures in the imprint line and is legally responsible for the contents of the paper. If the trend of publishing newspapers exclusively for making money, with no commitment to social responsibility continues, it needs to be considered whether the postal and other privileges such papers enjoy be withdrawn are supposed to fulfil a public service.

Television networks and stations are driven by concerns about advertising revenues and market shares, and so they are constantly creating and showing whatever is the hottest and latest issue or the newest trend. In the case of radio, since the MW airwaves have been overcrowded, the FM network has been established to perform the functions of local radio. However, the FM radio has become so much dominated by market forces that it has become almost an *electronic disco* for the urban youth.

Social Responsibility of Media

While it is difficult to stop the onward march of market forces, the challenge of growing commercialisation and commodification of media has to be met fairly and squarely. This can be done only if local communities, NGOs, media academics and concerned citizens encourage, promote and implement alternate media—community Radio, Rural Press, Franchise TV stations for meeting the cultural specific and relevant needs of the participating audience. Public Service Broadcasting has to become the corner stone of the National Media Policy and the Broadcasting Law—now on the anvil.

The Sengupta Committee, set up in December 1995, by the Ministry of Information and Broadcasting, to make recommendations regarding restructuring of Prasar Bharati observed : In the wake of influx of alien entertainment, directed to the top crust, the minority with growing purchasing power and propensity to spend, the significance of public service broadcasting needs no over-emphasis. The presence of mere frothy entertainment, fun and frolic can only amuse for a while but cannot meet the real desires of people unless the fare offered is imbued with social purpose. We believe broadcasting has a higher purpose than the constant drive to reach out to the largest possible number of people, flattening out in the process disparate audiences into a homo-geneous mass of buyers. Crass commercialisation hinders variety in approach and style, resulting in mere variation of the same theme. We are convinced that without statutory protection, public service broadcasting will be far too vulnerable, especially in a multi-channel scenario. Public service broadcasting needs to be structurally embedded to Prasar Bharati so that it becomes a source of enrichment and empowerment of the masses.

As a part of Public Service Broadcasting, setting up a net work of Community Radio stations would go a long way in promoting need-based, low cost, relevant and culturally compatible broadcasting programmes. Since, more than 70% of India's population is rural, and has poor access to media sources and decision-making processes, it would seem appropriate to initiate Community Radio in rural areas first. For example, a collaboration between local NGOs, Panchayati Raj and other community representatives such as women, farmers, small businesses, cultural groups and the youth, could establish a core operating committee. Such participation at the local level in media ownership and dissemination naturally leads to the expansion of public spaces in India. Ideally, Community Radio's essentially social nature can influence public opinion, create consensus, thus strengthening democracy by increasing community contact and increasing its input in decision-making processes.

It would also be essential to enforce vigorously the codes and guidelines evolved by professional bodies like Advertising Standards Council of India (ASCI). The practice of surrogate advertising by the liquor industry has come in for severe criticism by the advertising industry itself. In a seminar on "self-regulation or pre-censorship" held in Bombay in January 1995, the Chairman of Radeus Advertising K. Kurian said : By promoting their pro-ducts through surrogate advertising certain liquor manufacturers are destroying the credibility of advertising itself. He said that such a "con job" gave credence to the belief that advertising is the art of converting a complete lie into a half-truth.

It is heartening indeed to observe a senior advertising professional protesting against advertising malpractices indulged in by their own profession.

A young media researcher and reporter in USA, in his research study on social responsibility to news media pointed out the grave repercussions of junk journalism (Market-Driven Journalism : Let the Citizen Beware? John H. McManus). In India, however a Cable TV executive says : The design of our business is such that we can buy junk, brand it and sell it at a premium, *India Today*, 15 June 1996.

The tendency to market junk - or recycled junk, even if attractively packaged, has to be curbed.

REFERENCES

Agarwal, Amit (1996). Channels—An Awful Lot of Hoping, 15 June, *India Today*.

French, D. and Richards, M. (eds.) (1996). *Contemporary Television—Eastern Perspectives*. Sage Publications, New Delhi.

Gupta, V. S. and Rajeshwar Dyal (1996). *National Media Policy*, Concept Publishing Company, New Delhi.

Ministry of Information and Broadcasting (1996). Sengupta Committee Report, Government of India, New Delhi.

ELECTRONIC MEDIA

15

TELEVISION
Emerging Realities and Priorities

—GOPAL SAKSENA

Television has now come to be universally recognised as a medium of people. To be true to its form and spirit as such, two major factors call the shots for the box. These are the realities emerging in a society and the changing choices of its people for programmes to watch. Both these have to be fully reflected in the telecast material. To ensure that the programmes click with viewers fresh inputs of themes, formats, techniques and styles of presentation are a must for any television network.

The proliferation of the satellite channels and the expansion of cable television in India have in recent years radically changed the media scenario. The world at large appears to have been reduced to a virtual global village. The present TV audience in India can safely be assessed at over 400 million. But it is very heterogeneous, cosmopolitan and complex. Their regions, religions, languages, traditions, social attitudes, levels of comprehension, economic status and political affiliations (atleast inclinations)—are all very different and varying. Then, there is a sharp urban and rural divide.

Such contradictions abound and baffle the software planners of all networks, participating in the race for supremacy. Most of them, especially the Government-controlled National Television Authority i.e. Doordarshan, have to put out some sort of a compromised` dish, having `something for every one`. Naturally, it fails to satisfy many.

Of late, we have been passing through a swift transition—from `the established` to what is being experienced. With this change, are changing the very fundamentals of our life—our approach, flair, interests and of course, television viewing-patterns and prefe-rences. Caught up in this whirl-pool, modern man has no patience to soak-in and appreciate the on-going programmes. He wants to taste the new, racy, spicy and entertaining. This urge in him has been accentuated by the numerous channels, offering a varied fare. The viewer is feeling free from that old `have-it-or-leave-it` syndrome, that the lone Doordarshan had perpetrated for decades. Now the whole world is virtually at the door-steps of our drawing rooms.

Influence of Market Forces on Programming Strategies

Of course, many channels and many cable networks are operating these days. But each one has to fight a grim battle for survival. More so, because television needs huge investments on a long-term basis. Every single minute on the air costs money. The only way out for the channel owners or runners is to attract advertisements to go with their programmes. But unfortunately, the advertising revenue has not risen nor is likely to rise in the near future, in proportion to the telecast-time available on different channels. It has been fragmented.

The popularity of a programme virtually determines an advertiser's choice. The programme having higher TRP has more chances of having more ads. Advertising on television is a game of the survival of the fittest. Or say, the survival of the best software. The market forces shape and influence the programme strategies these days. What should go where and when are all decided according to the dictates of market forces. Quite some time back D. Sriram and Vishnu Mohan of Redifusion Precision Media, in their article, "Reworking the Media Strategy" published in the *Economic Times*, dated May 11, 1994, said :

> Today, as a result of the satellite television explosion, the very nature of media in India has changed. Consequently, the task of media planner is much more complicated. The homogeneity of television viewing has disappeared. Most of these multichannel households are in the urban centres which are the key markets for most advertisers.

According to S. Shetty, Senior Media Controller, Mudra Communications, one of India's top advertising agencies, advertisers will have to start now adjusting their strategies for using television according to the dictates of market. He said :

> Now, the emphasis has to shift from increasing reach to increasing frequency, identifying target groups specifically for each product. Then, different programmes would need to match a particular audience profile.

Considering the viewer-rating of various programmes, one fact emerges crystal clear : "TV for whom", and "for what"—are no more a simple question to answer. Not only Doordarshan's programme-planners, social-scientists or communicators, but even viewers do not precisely and critically know what to like and what to discard.

The present competition has brought about another change in the basics of television in this country. Universally regarded as a serious business of ideas and creativity, television has largely become a business of pure economics. Earlier concepts of its being a major source of education and information are no more valid. TV is shaping up primarily as a vehicle of entertainment. This is because the survival of different channels has become dependent upon advertisement revenue that they can generate through their programmes. The logic is simple. The entertainment-oriented shows alone can make the advertiser's message reach viewers. And, in this bargain, what viewers get are a large number of film-based shows. Particularly because such shows are easy to produce, cost less financially as well as creatively, and yet score high TRPs.

In the Chapter, 'Entertainment Redefined', the Joshi Working Group on Software for Doordarshan made some interesting observations. They thought it was the time that Doordarshan gave up its "pathetic reliance" on "debasing" commercial films. . . (made) "to a formula of sentimentality, melodrama, violence and sex", Chitrahaar and similar song and dance sequences (showing) "a man and a woman rolling on each other down a grassy slope . . . or dancers swinging hips and bosoms". . . or foreign serials ("irrelevant atrociously mindless and/or vulgar"). Instead, they wanted that "the rich heritage of country's folk and classical arts" must find a proper place in the software of Doordarshan.

By providing the opium-like addiction through seamy, sensual song and dance sequences from films in a number of programmes, good taste, inherent earlier in family viewing, has been ruthlessly violated. This has caused concern. Even the Parliament took exception to the programmes "now being seen in drawing room (having been) so pornographic that it was embarrassing to watch them with children sitting around." But the then Minister for Information and Broadcasting assured at that time that "there will be no compromise on the effort to rid Indian films of sex, violence and vulgarity." But as the things are now, there is not much of perceptible change in this regard.

Promoting Commercialisation

With the entertainment becoming the staple diet of television in India, commercialisation has got an out-of-way push and promotion. For our economy, this trend does not augur well. For, commercialisation leads to consumerism and consumerism leads to unwanted (and often undeserved) demands.

Now, a word about the changing concepts of advertising, especially in terms of advertising on television. I would like to quote from Encyclopaedia Britannica :

> The prices consumers pay are also an indicator of the value they place on the product, and value is something more than the sum total of all the production and marketing costs, as value to the consumer is the sum total of his perceptions of the product and the gratification he attaches to it. Anything that enhances his perceptions adds to the value.

Advertising is often credited for selling newer ideas and ideals, concepts and technologies. These trends refashion our attitudes to suit our changing economy and social ethos. Nelson's theory starts with the belief that consumers "have far less than perfect information about products . . . But consumers will respond to advertising only if it provides information to them at a lower cost than do alternate sources of information." This applies to both the developed and the developing countries.

Let us not forget that TV is a powerful medium. In India also, it is now within the reach of the poorest of the poor. In a society like ours, where three-fourths of people come from rural areas and 40 per cent of them live below poverty-line, indiscriminate advertising may prove harmful. Projecting on their sets the products, primarily relevant to urban elite, might create many a distortion in life of the less-favoured. For, they might ill-afford the newly created demands. We have to consciously keep this parameter in mind so as to avoid various social and economic tensions. Advertising will, therefore, have to be need-based, conforming to the basic value system of our society. Well, to accentuate desire beyond one's means is always suicidal.

The success of advertising depends on public confidence. And, nothing should be done which might impair this confidence. At the same time, advertising should not offend morality, decency, aesthetic perceptions and social susceptibilities of the people. It implies that advertising will have to go beyond 'glamour' or the concept of, what is generally called, 'show-biz'. It has to be in conformity with the social obligations, enjoined upon mass-media of our country. The market forces will continue to have tremendous impact on our television. It is for those responsible for running a television or cable network to withstand this pressure.

16

IMPACT OF MARKET FORCES ON SATELLITE AND CABLE TELEVISION

—UMA NARULA

The Indian media is currently revolutionised due to advance communication technologies, more so electronic media. We discuss about market forces which are responsible for revolutionising the electronic media—the satellite and cable television and the consequential changes, challenges and opportunities created by these market forces on the Indian media scenario. The consequential changes raise certain concerns and issues, pose challenges for media policy makers, practitioners, producers and consumers; and also create further opportunities or development in the varied associated media infrastructures.

Market Forces

There are three-fold salient internal factors conducive to expansion of satellite and cable T.V.

1. Market forces controlled by the government such as techno-policy of the government focusing on advance media technologies; and media policies of the government focusing on autonomy, privatization, commercialisation and the cut off point of social obligations for electronic media.
2. Market forces controlled by media practitioners and producers focusing on management of media; expansion of both hardware and software of cable television and satellites.

3. Consumers' (people, programmers, manufacturers) readiness for expansion and the priority given by consumers to expansion categories such as (i) type and content of focus of programmes, and (ii) willingness to pay for those products and services. The consumers (media practitioners, programmers, manufacturers, etc.) prioritize for certain class.

The globalization of the market forces in communication is the major external factor.

Both these external and internal market forces for expansion of satellite and television raise certain issues. These issues pose challenges and create further opportunities for development.

The market forces have both positive and negative impact on programmers (including all infrastructures), consumers and government. The technological development and its applications to media technologies, media technologies related industries focusing on expansion of satellites and cable television is far reaching. It gives better connectivity, quicker exposure to priorities and global exposure to issues. Further it gives impetus to media related peripheral industries, development of hardware and software for the same and development and utilization of human resources (use of personnel and talent).

Significant role is played in expansion and development by the techno-policies and media policies of a country and its related economic and political environment. Further, the dominant ideology of a country/society—whether pro-social, entertainment, educational, edu-entertainment labour saving, etc. have impact on expansion and development of media. Inspite of availability and access to advance technology; it is the application of these technologies that matters. Applications depend on techno, media policies and related economic and political factors, and dominant cultural ideology of the society.

The changing psyche of the consumers (people, programmers, manufacturers, media practitioners) is a significant market force in expansion and development of media. The consumer public wants more and varied content programmes as well more programme channels. Programmers produce more to satisfy the consumer public. There is competition in variety and contents of programmes, talent scouting and advertisements. Media manu-facturing industries develop through applications of advanced technologies as well as better technology delivery. The media practitioners set the agenda for the type and contents of programmes. The policy-makers set the agenda for applications of the technology.

The market force of globalization creates global information grid resulting in international networks, foreign cultural influx and influences. There is positive impact of globalization for cultural assimilation. Cultures have become more visible, vocal and global through exposure to media technologies. Barriers among nations are brought down historically, geographically, languagewise and culturally. Such diversity of exposures brings openness which modifies our perspectives to one another and awareness to changing world realities. These realities pertain to social structures, values, policies and human relationships. Foreign influences expose the diversity of cultural challenges. The policy makers, programmers and consumers cope with impact of diverse values, lifestyles and ways of life.

Hanson and Narula (1990) take a culture specific viewpoint of technology rather taking a global perspective (though the global exposures will be there and are inevitable). They argue that functions and gratifications of media technologies are not applicable the same way universally though the medium is universal. They must be adopted to the needs of the different cultures, acquired and introduced at different levels of variations.

The interplay of competition among all the above mentioned categories of market forces develop and expand satellites, cable television and its infrastructures through applications of advance technologies. This is likely to create better facilities and delivery to all class of consumers by encouraging related industries like advertisement, peripheral industries like cable operators, decoders, etc.

Opportunities, Issues and Concerns

The global programmes through cable and satellites T.V. expose viewers and consumers to diverse cultural values and structures and ways of life and patterns of life styles. The consumers have the opportunity to pick and choose the values, ways, styles and structures they want to adopt and assimilate in their own cultural ways and values. Some of these already get sublimely absorbed and further reinforced by frequent exposures to these programmes. It is argued that impact of negative/alien global values may erode our own cultural vitality and stability. The counter argument is that in today's era we are all multicultural and we all create our identities from these multicultural values. Whatever negative we pick from diverse cultures, it is what we want for ourselves. Therefore, the control has to be from within.

The ever increasing satellite services, cable television, and now digital television and multimedia in the offing will positively contribute to communication revolution but our second major concern is the social, economic and information stress, that these contributions may create.

There may be negative social impact from the perspective of individual, family, community, national and international interests. It will negatively affect the quality of life and activities of the individual family relationships, leisure time utilization and community based activities. The social system may suffer too by increasing the gap between the information rich and information poor, and more involvement through content, style and control of programmes.

We are concerned with the information stress that will be created by information load, information gap and the time and the facilities we need to enjoy and consume these facilities. This is likely to create social stress resulting in low leisure time activities, changing life styles, changing personal, social, and professional networks and less personal time and space. There will be economic stress as more facilities will incur more expenses.

Social, information and economic stress and overall time-sink with television may negate some of the positive points. But will this discourage expansion? Is it cost effective from social and economic point of view? The poser is social and economic cost effectiveness vis-a-vis television expansion in different societies. These two factors may ultimately restrict as well as balance the expansion of the satellites and television. Information is precious commodity. It is imperative in developing societies to make it cost effective both socially and economically by balancing the above mentioned two concerns.

Future Directions and Initiatives for Media

In the background of the opportunities, issues, and concerns raised by the above-mentioned market forces operating on the media scenario; it is imperative that media takes initiatives for utilization of these market forces.

(a) Information networks on media may be created but we control the range and the quantum of information; (b) give access, availability, and affordability of information to those for whom it is created; and (c) social accountability for information created and utilized by creating awareness among the disseminaters of such information, co-ordination among information networks both personal, social, professional and mechanical i.e. software, hardware, and human resources.

In order to ensure balanced attention and utilization to other media units, such as print, folk, etc. as in developing countries like India integrated media units coordinating with plural cultural identities and urban and rural identities are needed.

It is argued that at best currently the electronic media promotes consumerism which is unhealthy and unwanted. Advertisement with all its gimmicks is the arm that promotes it. We need advertising to give information, education (IEC), therefore, consumerism is unavoidable. The responsibility and social accountability is to control the consumerism created and promoted. It is the joint responsibility of policy makers, and consumers and their infrastructures.

There is double bind. Privatisation is encouraged for programme channels for cable television to ensure competition for improving quality of programmes. Most of these programmes aim at commercial revenue through advertisements and also provide heavy doses of entertainment to attract more viewers. Though more and more of privatization will be needed to ensure healthy competition, quality programmes and stimulation to produce more. Private initiative should be public service oriented. It is a must in developing countries. Government by privatization gives them more initiative for expansion and competition for quality. But there has to be rethinking of the role of government and private initiative. It changes through times, a constant dialogue is imperative. There will be market forces operative to protect private initiative, there will be competition and healthy market trends to expand. It is, however, essential not to ignore media ethics.

Through passage of time we will expand both the products and television services but we need to assume more of social responsibility not only for disseminating information and education but disseminating in the positive manner. There has been lot of campaign on T.V. about safe water being provided in the villages but recently when due to low maintenance and negligènce lead was eroding in the water pipes nobody informed them about the unsafe water.

Control of market forces is essential through regulation and regulatory mechanism to follow the planning, policy decisions and guidelines. Human perceptions and media scenario will be changing due to socio-economic change, technology revolution, liberalization and also due to the compulsions of the bureaucratic environments but what we need is an umbrella organisation for advocacy of consumers, media professionals, media industries and other infrastructure.

Future Trends and Emerging Media Scenario

We can foresee the future trends in the media expansion and development which suggests a major shift from purely entertainment oriented programmes to infotainment, multiculturalism, expansion to multi-channels to cater to these growing needs; and privatization of these channels. This shift suggests intense competition among the various market forces affecting the media scenario.

Our concern, poser is : What new market forces will ›merge? How will the interplay of old and new market forces, and their supportive roles will shape and reshape the market forces and the media scenario? Who will benefit most the consumers or the producers? Will conflicting demands of marketing forces vis-a-vis consumers and producers pose dilemmas.

The differing market forces will create pressures on the media and the emerging market forces, consumers' needs, demands and trends will demand focused television programme channels such as educational, agriculture, business, etc. It is assumed that as more and more information load will be there, the consumer will become selective in style, type and contents of channels and programmes.

Let us treat the consumer as human and not as mechine

though in future we may have the technical capabilities of disseminating information like machine. We also assume that the future social and media dynamics may change. Rather, either the media or the audience setting the agenda; it is more likely that the agenda of both will coexist and operate. This is likely to create 'public space' and 'communication space' for people.

REFERENCES

Hanson, Jarice and Narula, Uma (1990). *New Communication Technologies in Developing Countries.* Lawrence Erlbaum Associate, N. J.

Narula, Uma (1996). *Cultural Diffusion : Dynamics and Challenges* (in press).

17

ELECTRONIC MEDIA AND PUBLIC SERVICE BROADCASTING

—NANDINI PRASAD

As a part of worldwide phenomenon, mass media in India too have experienced tremendous technological changes in the last decade or so. A number of new technologies have resulted in the creation of a stream of products and services which are called "new" information and communication technologies. A remarkable feature of these technologies is their often converging relationship with each other. One also observes a very rapid spread of these new technologies within India and across the globe. Since these new communication technologies are capital-intensive and require massive investments, the media players in the field, be it in the private sector or the government, have to depend on commercial revenue which each medium is capable of raking in. Consequently, in order to make any media activity a "commercially viable" proposition, choices and preferences of the people are given uppermost priority. What people "want" to read in newspapers, see on television and in films, and listen to over the radio is made available to them by the media owners and their managers. The main objective is to make continuous efforts to increase readership/viewership/listenership so that revenue of advertisements could be attracted. What they "ought" to read in newspapers, television and in films and listen over the radio becomes a casuality in this market-driven media situation. Commercial advertising dominates the media and the aspect of social responsibility of media takes a back-seat. Advertisers are targeting the sizeable middle class which is estimated to be around 240 million. It is also growing at the rate of 10 per cent per year. The advertisers are aware of the middle-classes' keenness to acquire all sorts of consumer durables. Consequently, middle-class consumerism is greatly stimulated by the media—print, television and radio in particular.

My intention is not to run down the role of advertising in society and also in the expansion and growth of media. The way advertisers need different media channels, media also depend largely on advertising support. It is very difficult to delink media totally from commercial advertising. In India's mixed economy, more so after economic liberalisation, advertising has acquired the status of an inevitable reality. Not only has it come to stay—it has become an integral part of the economic and social life in India.

When advertising has become such a major force because of its pervasive and persuasive character, its social responsibility becomes a matter of concern. Its contents and forms, as used by the advertising agency have become a subject of fierce controversy.

Admittedly, the advertiser's aim is to sell, but at what, and at whose cost? How concerned is the advertiser about the direction which society's value system must take? These are some of the questions that need to be kept in mind while discussing the issue of market-driven media.

Television

The advent of satellite and cable television has led to proliferation of television channels—mostly in the private sector. Their main concern is to earn as much revenue as possible through commercial advertising which is directly related to its size of viewers. Private channel operators know that the easiest and quickest way to build up, increase and sustain its viewers is by providing just "entertainment" for which they rely heavily on films and films based programmes, tele-serials, game-shows, chat-shows, etc. Indian films industry provides substantial proportion of private channels' programming. Entertainment, more entertainment and even more entertainment seems to be the key to success for private TV channels. Their target is urban-middle-class population with buying capacity which will bring in more and more of advertising revenue. Providing useful information and education for the development of the society is not on their agenda.

Doordarshan, in its endeavour to compete with the onslaught of private satellite channels, be they foreign or Indian, has also resorted to adding heavy doses of all kinds of entertainment programmes. Although, it still continues to telecast news and current affairs programmes and programmes which are informative and educative, such programmes are telecast at times when viewership is low. On the other hand, commercially sponsored entertainment programmes are shown at "prime-time" which is actually the time when people are watching television. Doordarshan is caught in a dilemma as to how to compete with private channels and also to perform its role as a public broadcasting service. The market forces are compelling Doordarshan to show more of what people want to see rather than what they ought to see.

Looking at the figures of Doordarshan's income from commercials, the picture becomes clearer. The growth of television in terms of receiving sets as well as of commercial revenue earned by Doordarshan has been spectacular. As on December 1982, the total number of TV homes was 20,60,727 which has risen to 45,68,300 (29,97,200 in urban areas and 15,71,100 in rural areas) in December, 1994 for which figures are available. This must have increased further in the past one and half year. Doordarshan's commercial revenue has gone up by leaps and bounds since the introduction of commercials on 1 January, 1976.

The social cost of the increasing commercial revenue in terms of its effect on popular taste, social order and the moral health of the nation is incalculable. The Working Group on Doordarshan Software recalled the criticism by the Second Press Commission, in its report of April 1982, of certain types of advertisements in newspapers which promoted sexism and a consumerist culture. The Group pointed out that government-run Doordarshan should be even more conscious of its social responsibility than the privately owned Press. The Press Commission had said : It was recognised that classified advertisements relating to employment, matrimony, housing and the like serve a useful function, but a considerable part of display advertising was prodigal and had to be curtailed. The glossy magazines and the glossiest of advertise-ments in the Press—of jeans and soft drinks, cigarettes and cosmetics, air travel or entertainment in five-star hotels—are directed at the newly affluent and their children. We are of the view that the Press must address itself to the question of what contribution it is making to

DOORDARSHAN'S INCOME FROM COMMERCIALS

Year	Rs. million
1976-77	7.7
1977-78	20.7
1978-79	49.7
1979-80	61.6
1980-81	80.8
1981-82	112.7
1982-83	158.9
1983-84	179.9
1984-85	314.3
1985-86	602.0
1986-87	933.1
1987-88	1363.0
1988-89	1612.6
1989-90	2101.3
1990-91	2538.5
1991-92	3006.1
1992-93	3602.3
1993-94	3729.5
1994-95	3980.0

the strengthening of the moral fabric of society and discouraging the trend towards conspicuous and excessive consumption which a developing country can ill afford . . . There has been an increasing tendency to exploit sex appeal. The exploitation of the female form in commercial advertising promotes the notion of women as sex objects and runs contrary to the news items and articles which many newspapers carry in support of treating women as equals and respecting their personality as individuals endowed with as much human worth as males.

The Software Group also recalled the decision made by the

Indonesian President in 1981 to discontinue commercial advertising on Indonesian television because of its socially destabilising effect through the generation of wants not matched by the means of satisfying them. In view of all this, some members of the Software Group were of the view that Doordarshan should altogether discontinue commercial advertising and the only 'messages' in advertising style on Doordarshan henceforth should be public service messages such as for the promotion of savings, family planning, health practices, girls' education, blood donation, environment, traffic safety, and the like. According to these members of the Software Group, it was absurd for the Government with one hand to stoke the fires of consumerism through its media and with the other hand to try and contain the consequences in terms of crime and corruption.

"While appreciating and respecting the concerns felt by these colleagues", the report said, "the majority of us in the Working Group are of the view that advertising is inseparable from a modern industrial economy in which production is not organised locally to meet locally felt needs but is based on a national and an international market. However, we are emphatically of the view that advertising should not promote male chauvinism and sexism."

In view of the fact that the time most sought after by commercial advertisers was during and around the telecast of feature films and film-based programmes, the report said : "Our recommendation, in the chapter on Entertainment, of a reduction in the time devoted to such programmes may possibly, but not necessarily, lead to a drop in earnings from commercials. Since the advertiser is interested in audience rating and not in the nature of the programme that attracts high viewing, it is upto Doordarshan to offer attractive programmes of excellent content during part of the time now being applied to films and film-based programmes, much of them in poor taste and socially harmful. If indeed there should be a drop in commercial revenue, it should be accepted as the price for correcting Doordarshan's wrong practice hitherto in the selection of commercial films and in the compilation of song-and-dance sequences therefrom. Doordarshan is not in the business of television for raking in the maximum revenue from commercials; advertisements are incidental to its essentially educative role as a publicly owned mass medium."

In its race to sustain, and subsequently keep on increasing its viewership, Doordarshan has fallen prey to market-driven TV situation and seems to be quite satisfied with its success in earning more and more commercial revenue. A public service broadcasting channel is no different from private channels whose sole aim is to maximise their profits. As such, all TV channels, including Doordarshan, are governed by the forces of demand (of their viewers) and supply (of entertainment programmes). Now, can a country like India afford the use of the most powerful medium like TV only for entertainment purposes?

Radio

As compared to television, radio has a much wider reach in both urban and rural areas, but more in the rural areas. With the expansion and growth of television since the 80s, people in urban areas almost completely switched over to television, abandoning radio, which they were earlier using as a source of entertainment, as well as information. Because of the high cost of purchasing a television set and also the non-availability and shortage of electricity in rural areas, radio still commands a sizeable listenership in rural areas. All India Radio has been struggling against the onslaught of television in various ways. However, most of their efforts are again targetted at urban listeners which could help in bringing of commercial revenue. AIR's income from commercials may not be galloping like that of Doordarshan, their endeavour is to introduce programmes (like FM channel) which will increase their commercial revenue. In fact, AIR had negated its very objective of being a vehicle for providing information and education for overall development of society by going commercial and starting Vividh Bharati channels which provided mostly entertainment programmes with film music. The concept of local broadcasting which has been given more hype than put into practice seems to have been relegated to the background. Although AIR claims that they are broadcasting adequate number of instructional programmes, socially relevant messages and programmes for specialised audiences like women, youth, armed forces, children, etc. but who listens to these programmes is a different question. Firstly, these programmes are broadcast at times when the listenership may be insignificant and secondly the quality of such programmes is not good enough to generate listenership. As such, AIR seems to be mainly concerned about the entertainment programmes for which commercial sponsorship and advertisement support is easily available. What goes into these programmes is ultimately decided by the sponsors of these programmes. Like television, radio is also caught in this vicious circle of listener's desires and advertisers interest to fulfil those desires for their own profits.

Newspapers—A Commodity?

The proprietor of a leading chain of newspapers openly declared in his meeting with the chief editor and his other journalist associates that his newspaper is a 'commodity' and he would adopt all hardsell marketing techniques to promote this commodity. Not only that he insisted that the daily editorial meeting will include his business manager also. He surpassed all limits by insisting that his business manager will write the editorial for the union budget which was presented around that time. The journalist fraternity, within that newspaper, and elsewhere too, were deeply shocked and the chief editor, alongwith some of his close associates immediately resigned in disgust. Journalists working in other newspapers were also alarmed because their proprietors were also businessmen first and businessmen last. They also knew that this kind of a situation could take place in their newspaper any time. Ultimately, most of them reconciled to the fact that journalistic inputs into the newspaper will take a back seat and the commercial interest of increasing circulation and advertising revenue will be in the forefront. So much for the value of journalists role in setting the agenda for the nation, shaping and building the society.

The story goes further. The same proprietor, on the advice of his business managers, reduced the price of the paper by half which triggered a price war all over the country among major newspapers. In the case of big dailies, loss of revenue by reduction in price was not only covered by the increase in advertisement revenue due to increased circulation, but the overall profits increased tremendously. Ultimately, it was the medium and small newspapers which were hit by this price-war as they had no scope for reducing their price.

These days, newspapers are focusing on "infotainment", making newspapers more entertaining. Readers are provided special supplements everyday. Apparently, news and views are becoming incidental. It is only the profit motive which is of utmost importance.

The Issues

In this situation of market-driven media the target group is restricted to urban middle and upper class and the majority of the country's population is non-existent. On the other hand, the media inputs, in fact, generate tensions among the have-nots as it increases desires and aspirations which is beyond their means.

The other point is that the government seems to have given tacit approval to the market forces governing the media. First, the government introduced economic liberalisation inviting multinationals and foreign investors, not only in the core sectors, but also in the consumer products area. Obviously, the investors will seek the help of media for promoting their products through intensive advertising. And, therefore, the media contents are dictated by the advertisers.

It is understandable that the profit motive is uppermost in the minds of media owners, practitioners and investors in the private sector. But what about the public service broadcasting networks of Doordarshan and All India Radio, whose sole responsibility is to achieve the objectives of a welfare state.

18

ELECTRONIC MEDIA
Pace and Direction

—S. KASBEKAR

Communication media explosion is here to stay. In this Age of Communication and Information, media is the single most important factor which contributes to inform, educate and entertain the public. It must also satisfy the growing need of the public for more knowledge, more immediate news as well as more wholesome entertainment.

Print Media

In the overall scenario, print media is going through a difficult time due to the viable competition offered by electronic media. The print media has some inherent qualities which can be summarised as follows : This media provides a wider variety of news and information as compared to the electronic media and can also present far more details than the electronic media. Secondly, human beings today must assimilate an astounding amount of information to keep pace with a rapidly changing world. They do this by continuously programming their brains which can be compared to a highly sophisticated computer. The printed word can be used far more efficiently in this process. For instance, advertisements in newspapers concerning insurance, issue of bonds, or employment are more effective.

Newspapers have the advantage of presenting information, developing issues and motivating action at the local level. They can give meaning and perspective to community life not possible through the other media.

Technological Revolution

The printed word has changed drastically from the days of Johannes Guttenberg, the craftsman from Mainz, Germany, who invented the movable type and revolutionised the future of the printed word. Gutenberg gave us letterpress printing, followed by mechanical typesetting, basically the invention of Monotype (1886) and Linotype (1887).

Then came a technological revolution in the form of phototypesetting, which displaced almost 75 per cent of hot metal composition. Today phototypesetting has come to stay. These sweeping changes have started encouraging new concepts and new modes of communication. These could be summarised as follows :

1. Electronic document creation and editing which includes word processing and computerised text editing.
2. Phototypesetting with a wide variety of direct entry, on-line and off-line computerised systems.
3. Electronic communication including electronic mail, electronic publication and electronic journals.
4. Use of Internet for information, the use of new recording storage, and retrieval systems like holographic storage, bubble memories, etc.

What has been the result of all this? Today, with the introduction of the computer and electronic media, the fundamental product is a database. This can be used very flexibly for a variety of purposes.

This development of electronic literature makes it possible for collection of information, updating, revision and reproduction so flexible that it is easy to store, produce and reproduce a vast amount of literature in a short span of time.

It is now possible to use the database stored in a computer at one spot and transfer, with ease, this information to another spot. For example, a journalist can prepare his article on the word processor at home and this can be transferred to magnetic disk. The data can be transferred to a printing press far away through telephone lines. The printer, using an interface, can transfer the data to the phototypesetter which produces the author's copy in the form of a film negative or a photographic paper positive in the shape of final page proofs. By this means, the publisher and typesetting operators are both eliminated and the author directly produces the printed word. The printer carries out only the plate making and printing on the press.

In India, the electronic newspaper is not yet a reality; but it has come to stay in countries like the United States of America. This newspaper brings information to the very doorsteps of the subscriber. "The Columbia Despatch" became the first newspaper in the United States to go electronic on 1st July, 1980. The subscriber has a television terminal in his house connected to the newspaper office through telephone lines. The subscriber dials the newspaper office and turns on the video terminal for the latest edition of the newspaper to appear on his screen. If he wants any particular portion of the newspaper, like the sports page, entertainment or market reports, he can call it upon the screen by pressing the coded keys. This is the electronic newspaper which has eliminated the printed word.

Magazines have undergone a revolution in recent years. Today, there are magazines in almost all subjects. The market is flooded with them. Magazine audiences are very specific and target audiences are also easy to identify. Yet, magazines have changed drastically in the last few years due to market compulsions. As Ms. Sathya Saran, Editor, "*Femina*", put it succinctly, "Magazines now have to be visually exciting to compete with the electronic media". It is not enough for her magazine to highlight issues of importance to women. They need to add glossy colourful fashion pages and display hi-tech products which have visual appeal. Magazine covers are, therefore, getting bolder, louder and exotic. They need to arrest, hold and ensure the customer.

A market compulsion is Photo Journalism. Photographs have their own distinctive place in "dressing up" the page of a newspaper or magazine but today's photo journalism has come a long way : With the still video camera, editors can now have on their desks, ready for press, a picture shot across the country minutes earlier. The secret. The camera does all its work electronically. Film processing and print developing have been eliminated. In fact, there is no film. In Canon's still video camera, the light is gathered by a silicon chip. On the chip are 600,000 tiny photo receptors that capture the scene as individual elements of brightness and colour called pixels. The image is converted by the chip to electrical impulses and transferred within the camera to a small floppy disk. Plugging the disk into viewing equipment, the photographer can screen and select the best shots, then the picture data are transmitted by photoline and satellite.

Electronic Media

This can broadly be classified as Audio Media and Audío-Video Media. The radio is the single most effective audio media. Recognised as a Companion Medium, the radio has some important characteristics :

1. It has a world wide network, not hampered by barriers—physical, political or racial.
2. It is easy to carry around : The farmer can carry it to the field, the mechanic to his shop.
3. It is relatively of low cost. Most average, middle class persons own a radio set.
4. It is a one-way medium.
5. Specialised programmes can be easily slotted for women, children, farmers, industrialists, music programmes, etc.
6. In India, the radio is owned and managed by the government. This makes it a "limited" media, in a sense.

The estimated radio households in India amount to 104 million, while the estimated radio sets in India are 111 million. The penetration of radio is to 81 per cent of the urban households and 68 per cent of the rural households.

Today, AIR broadcasts approximately 75 hours of programmes daily in 23 foreign languages. Strengthening is being accomplished through four SW transmitters of 250 KW each and two of 500 KW each. Thus, modernisation by introduction of the state of the art technology in all spheres of broadcasting is on the anvil. Digital technology is being introduced by the use of the compact disc system.

Yet, radio is viewed as the poorer brother of Doordarshan. AIR itself requires promotion.

This reminds me of a similar situation at a private radio

station KNX in U.S.

KNX decided to poke a little fun at itself and the listeners as well, hoping to generate a new interest in the format. The key to the strategy was to use puns. These were aired with suitable musical interludes.

"Archeologists dig our coverage.
Artists brush up on our news.
Policemen find our news arresting.
Sailors like our anchor men.
Housewives are at home with us . . . ."

The effect was immediate. These 10 seconds spots created humour and garnered response from the audience. Over 5300, on-air suggestions poured in.

Thus, AIR needs to revamp its style and content.

Television

While radio is a theatre of the mind, television is a theatre of home. TV is a glamour medium, family medium. TV has entered our homes— not only our drawing rooms, but also our bedrooms.

The television medium has certain characteristics. It requires a complex and formal organisation. It has a large audience belonging to different groups, classes, cities and nations. There is no instantaneous feedback. Distribution is free, unstructured. Audiences are heterogeneous.

It is a unique invention of modern society. Television has come to provide "the dominant cultural environment for much of the world", according to Marlene Cuthbert.

The Indian Readership Survey (IRS), billed as the largest and most comprehensive study of its kind in the world, has come up with a definitive outline of media habits, demographic patterns and income and spending habits in both urban and rural India. The survey undertaken by the Media Research Users Council covered 1.64 lakh people across 573 towns and 2,056 villages in all Indian states. Twenty-two per cent of those surveyed have access to the press, 43 per cent to television and 22 per cent to radio. For the first time, children above 12 years and not 15 years have been included in the survey.

Advertising Industry

The advertising industry is expected to grow 30 per cent this year. But the print media is feeling the pinch because, financial and corporate advertising, which accounts for 30-35 per cent of its total advertising revenue, is down to 20-25 per cent.

With the primary market in the doldrums, some Rs. 400 crore of new issue ads, which are primarily in the print media, have not come in, at the same time the new multinationals are spending more on marketing rather than advertising.

Add to this the following figures : The advertising expenditure in India crossed the Rs. 1,500 crore mark in 1990. TV's share of advertising billing has increased from Rs. 11 crores in 1981 to Rs. 254 crores in 1990.

Channel Explosion

While considering television, we cannot ignore the channel explosion :

1991	1992	1993	1994	1995
DD-1	STAR Plus	Jain TV	Raj TV	BI TV
DD-2	Prime Sports	ATN	JJ TV	YES
	PTV	SUN TV	DD-4	DISCOVERY
	BBC	ASIA TV	GEC	EL-TV
	CNN	UDAYA TV	GEMINI	SONY
	Zee TV	(15 Channels)	STAR Movies	ESPN
	Chinese		(30 Channels)	TNT
	Channel V			DD CNN
	(10 Channels)			DD INDIA
				SUN MUSIC
				SUN MOVIE
				ZEE CINEMA
				MOVIE CLUB
				(44 Channels)

There is no doubt a mind boggling number of channels, yet, we must not lose sight of the fact that Doordarshan covers 85 per cent by population and 68 per cent by area. The number of television homes which have an access to Doordarshan is 45.7 million of which 30 million are urban households, while 15.7 million are rural households. On the other hand, satellite television has 44 channels today. The number of cable and satellite homes is about 16 million only which is much less when compared to those who have an access to Doordarshan.

All this proliferation by the electronic media brings us to some important points :

1. Firstly, is all this media-potential being used for development or for mere entertainment?
2. Are media restricting themselves when it comes to violence and sex or do market considerations override all this?
3. Is television a controlled intervention which is having an uncontrolled effect?
4. Since DD alone earned a vast amount of money from commercials amounting to almost Rs. 3,980 in 1994-95, is the advertiser going to rule when it comes to electronic media?

These questions can only be partially answered today.

Yet, conclusively we can say that the spread of electronic media is having far reaching consequences, some of which are not even being understood today. The print media is here to stay but it has to change drastically as the market demands. Radio needs considerable changes, especially at the programming level.

REFERENCES

Cuthbert, Marlene (*AEJAC Journal*, Vol. 5, 1993) Post Invasion TV in Grenada : Grenadian Culture and Reagan's TV Gift, pp. 71.

Life "150 Years of Photography". "Pictures that make a Difference". *The Future, Time & Life Building*, Rockfeller Centre, New York, pp. 105.

The Times of India, 17 March 1991.

Wolseley, E. Roland. Understanding Magazines. The Iowa State University Press, Ames, Iowa, USA, pp. 16.

19

MEDIA IN CHANGING MARKET ENVIRONMENT

—ASHOK KUMAR PANDA

The industrial and economic institutions developed through years of insulation in India have now been exposed to external forces. There has been a new awakening for the Private Sector and the Public Sector is also much different to what it was a decade back and is fast changing its priorities. The forces of free market economy and competition have been let loose and the existing institutions have also been making all out efforts to face the new reality. The scale of this transformation as well as the pace of change engulfing the socio-economic fabric of our country does not have a parallel in the history of modern India. These revolutionary changes obviously have special significance for the media as well, which has also undergone a rapid transformation over the past decade.

It has been rightly said that the concept of developed and developing nations has now turned out to be information-rich and information-poor. A nation which is not able to keep pace with the changes remains poor while nations which are able to meet the new challenges and changes become affluent and developed.

In fact, developed and developing nations are often separated by a wide gap in terms of access to the most advanced mass communication technologies.

Asia represents one of the most important emerging markets in the world and is seen today as the continent of the next century, as a region of rising incomes, changing lifestyles and growing influence. The development of the communications infrastructure in Asia will no doubt play an important part in

Asia's phenomenal growth. And it is firmly believed that it will continue to play an important role in shaping Asia's social, political, cultural and economic life.

The communication industry in Asia is increasingly characterised by expansion and change. Communication is now the fastest growing industry in the region. Major players and new products are entering the market at a mind boggling pace, keeping up with the rapid developments in the industry.

Mass media in the Indian context has developed over centuries and has been able to carve a niche for itself as a matured, seasoned and comparatively independent institution. It has stood its ground through rough weather and gained strength through periods of social turmoil. Now this institution has also been influenced by recent changes in thinking and the fall-outs of the process of liberalisation.

India is not only the seventh largest economy in the world with a wide and diversified base in manufacturing and infrastructure sectors but also lately there has been a noticeable change in the attitude towards foreign direct investment.

Not very long back we had before us a smaller world a limited number of newspapers and periodicals with cognisable circulation and readership. We had the Doordarshan as the omnipresent electronic media. Anyone with some experience in the profession knew exactly what to do in a specific situation—like what all newspapers to choose for an advertising campaign or to find a slot on Doordarshan's prime time. Similarly, whom to approach for press briefings. Those simple equations are changing and changing at a rate much faster than at times we can comprehend. Apart from this, there has been a sea change in technology that has its bearing on corporate communications.

There was time when it was rare to come across an Indian company or a product in the international publication. But of late the scene seems to have changed. Many companies both in the private as well as in the public sector have been now persistently using these expensive magazines.

New World of Communication

In fact, even in India there has been a perceptible internationalisation of the society. The communicator needs to change his mind set in order to ensure a smooth entry into the new world of communication. It is first of all essential to build up a good data bank about every aspect of the profession vis-a-vis the needs and requirement of the organisation. This involves continuous monitoring of the media and changes that keep on taking place. With the multiplicity of satellites in sub-continent, there has been an improvement in the alternatives to choose but at the same time one confronts the problem of studying the viewership and exposure pattern for different alternatives.

Although there is an increase in choices there comes the problem of expenses and budgeting for advertising campaigns. Similarly, in the print media also the choices are gradually increasing. With many organisations now trying to find outlets abroad it has been pertinent to pick up specific foreign publications for advertising. Here again the cost factor has also to be examined as the expenses are likely to mount. Keeping the entire picture in mind one needs to fall back on authentic data and support from more professional advertising agencies.

The computer as a means of sending and receiving information has caught the people's imagination. Computer-mediated communication is becoming increasingly popular because of its speed, convenience, low cost and ability even to reach inaccessible pockets.

The number of people using computers is growing at a rapid pace. Newsweek estimated that by late 1995 in the United States above 37 million people aged 16 or older had access to the world wide web and were using the Internet on an average of five and half hours per week. Other nations are also adding networks at a rapid rate.

Barnes and Greller defined computer-mediated communication (CMC) as "when people use computer-networked systems to communicate to other people or to small groups of people". According to Rice and Case Computer-mediated communication has the potential to extensively affect social change and organisational structures and therefore "designers, vendors, organisational managers, and users alike are becoming more aware of the need to understand and, where possible, control these inputs".

Electronic mail is a well established channel of CMC. Garton and Wellman define E-mail as entering, storing, processing, distributing and receiving digitized communication through telecommunications network, E-mail offers fast, dyadic or multiple connections in a textual form that can be stored and manipulated and is not dependent on users being connected at the same place or time.

Television broadcasting and viewing in India have changed so much in the recent past, that the dynamics of the early period is no more relevant. Like many developed nations India has also started giving special emphasis to education and business programmes. It has also been successful in taking a major chunk of the advertisement revenue which was earlier mostly confined to the print media.

A big change in the newspaper environment is also imminent. With the electronic newspaper, the information and news function will be greatly enhanced. This will happen by systematizing the news and breaking out information by topic, subject and interest area. Further, it will add to speed in delivery of information and convenient electronic editing.

Another area which is becoming increasingly popular more so in India are the special features on specific subjects. Here the products are not only advertised but also dealt in news or story form for the audience to have adequate information about the company and its products. Many organisations prefer to participate in these special features because of the publicity their product enjoys.

Readers usually look for the news and not the advertising. With publicity one can be part of the news.

When the audience reads or views a product as news, there is an implied third party endorsement. The manufacturer and the public are the first two parties. The news people are the third party. Though publicity delivers the message and selects the medium, but unlike advertising, must filter its message through a reporter.

Further, it may not be always possible to be part of the publicity but possible to be part of the advertisement media within one's budget. Advertising also has the advantages of speed, timing, selectivity, definite delivery, completeness, accuracy and economy.

Technological Developments

With the world turning into a small global village, how fast and in what form the product/idea is available is the big question. The current technological developments which are leading to the convergence and integration of the telecommunications, computing and media industries are raising high expectations as to the sharing of knowledge and the fostering of intellectual co-operation.

It should, therefore, be a challenge also for the affluent nations to look for solutions to the priority needs of the underprivileged.

The customers approach in communication is just as vital as in any product marketing. Here the relevant information is the basic product, how effectively its delivered is the packaging, how easily the customer can get the information is the price the customer is willing to pay for the product and where he can get the information is the efficiency of the distribution system.

There is no denying the fact that media development is an essential instrument of social, political and economic development. To develop the society one must also develop the media. For a democratically-oriented society, it is essential to give people access to news and relevant information, be it for social upliftment or economic development.

PROCEEDINGS

20

PROCEEDINGS OF THE REGIONAL SEMINARS AND THE NATIONAL COLLOQUIUM

—V. S. GUPTA

REGIONAL SEMINARS

Hyderabad, 29-30 June 1996

The first Regional Seminar on Media and Market Forces—Challenges and Opportunities, was organised at Hyderabad on 29-30 June 1996. Delivering the presidential address at the inaugural session, the eminent Telugu writer and veteran journalist, P. Venkateshwara expressed his deep distress at the newly emerging trends in the contemporary media. He said : In order to combat the rising trend of commercialization of media and consequent debasement of Indian cultural traditions by market forces, it was essential that the journalism and media professionals be made aware of the impending danger facing the society at present. The former Vice-Chancellor, Dr. B. R. Ambedkar Open University, Prof. S. Bashiruddin said that there was an imperative need for encouraging public service programmes in areas like physical fitness, nutrition, immunization, etc. Alongwith liberalization of the media, the market forces should also pay attention to these aspects of human society, otherwise there would be a divide between the consuming classes and the deprived classes.

Prof. Bashiruddin added that a balance should be struck between advertising messages and analytical programmes or features in the media. Indian media has not yet been aware of this state of equilibrium. The literacy rate has been hardly 60 per cent or less for a national average and in some regions less than 50 per cent. The TV image or audio programmes on radio become a substitute for reality. In the absence of interactive TV, the programmes are originating to meet local news. Most of the audiences are given continuous entertainment. The advertising amount spent could surely provide social marketing of environment, health, education, nutrition and other areas. As the Indian press has no censorship and is free, there are to be some regulations or broad consensus in terms of news, views, features and advertising contents. Otherwise, the common man is not benefitted in terms of awareness of issues such as consumer rights, human rights, health and education welfare measures, etc. The experience of some of the advanced countries such as Japan, US, Germany, France, England, has been that while entertainment needs are met, the people's right to information and analysis of event affecting families and society are also given equal importance. A market-driven media can make everything consumer friendly but packaging of news is not the same as packaging of consumer products. It has to be objective, accurate, and relevant to the audiences' needs and aspirations.

Making a strong plea for public service broadcasting, Prof. Bashiruddin said that Public Service Broadcasting/advertising or features have not yet surfaced in the Indian media as in the case in Japan, US and other countries where large corporations produce features on cancer, AIDS, physical fitness programmes, nutrition, immunising and other social beneficial measures through social marketing of ideas, the Indian media should also take initiative in channelising advertising revenue on above lines. Alongwith the liberalisation of the media, the market forces should be attentive to these aspects of the human society in India.

AMIC's Country Representative, Prof. V. S. Gupta in his presentation said that India was increasingly becoming the playing field of the world's biggest media players for the share of its unregulated 15 million home cable TV market.

Ms. Sucharita S. Eashwar, Executive Director, Madhyam Communication, Bangalore, said that contemporary media is technology-driven and capital-intensive. It is linked with multi-national and trans-national corporations. She stressed the importance of people centred projects and alternative media including community and local radio stations which were relevant to the needs of the people living in small towns and villages.

FES Media Representative, Mr. Rajeshwar Dyal, in his presentation, said that development—the main objective of Doordarshan, which was enshrined as its basic policy, has been relegated to the background. The one and only concern of Doordarshan these days is to garner as much advertising revenue as possible, which was a retrograde step.

Patna, 27-28 July 1996

Since the information technology is developing very fast and communication is instantaneous in the contemporary media scenario, it is easier to get information from the west in a short span of time as compared to the places in the interior of states like Bihar. This observation was made by the Resident Editor of the *Times of India*, Patna edition, Mr. Uttam Sengupta, while addressing the inaugural session of the Regional Seminar on Media and Market Forces—Challenges and Opportunities, held at Patna on 27-28 July 1996. He regretted that the market forces have put a premium on entertainment and persons occupying central positions in the State and the Union Governments have not been able to pay attention to serious issues like land reforms and development issues. The newspaper reporting is becoming more dominated by political issues and social issues are being neglected.

In her paper, Media Analyst, Ms. Nandini Prasad stressed the need that Doordarshan and Akashvani should increasingly resort to public service broadcasting so as to achieve the objectives of a welfare state. She said that state owned electronic media had become a victim of emerging market forces and by emulating the private media, it had abandoned the role of social responsibility.

Doordarshan correspondent and media educator, Mr. Snehasis Sur said that challenges and opportunities will go side by side in the field of media and the market forces will play a determining role. However, the media professionals and planners should increasingly play a decisive role in the future of the media in our country.

The AMIC Zonal Representative, Mr. Ashok Kumar Panda, in his paper—Media in Changing Market Environment, said that television broadcasting and viewing in India have changed so much in the recent past, that the dynamics of the early period is no more relevant. Like many developed nations, India has also started giving special emphasis to education and business programmes. It has also been successful in taking a major chunk of the advertisement revenue which was earlier mostly confined to the print media.

A live discussion was held on the role of alternative media in the wake of liberalisation on the second day of the seminar. The panelists who participated in the discussion included the Secretary of Institutional Finance, Mr. P. P. Sharma, freelance journalist, Mr. Frank Krishnar and TV correspondent, Mr. Sudhanshu Ranjan.

Speaking on the occasion, Mr. Sharma said that media should be used as a facilitator and communicator for bridging the gap between the urban and the rural masses. They should project the real life image of a significant part of Indian population of Bihar that comprises 10 per cent of the total population of this country. Mr. Sharma lamented that a sum of over Rs. 300 crores public money is being invested in non-banking company every year. Such disclosures should be made in the larger public interests.

According to the Senior Development Executive of SRC-PCU and the Saminar Coordinator Ms. Sujata Sharma, the unprecedented growth in media industry and particularly in the electronic and satellite communication, witnessed during the recent years in India, had transformed the media scenario in the country as never before. Moreover, in the wake of economic liberalisation, the market forces are increasingly getting to be a determining factor. This had, as a result, also led to a change in the psyche of the consumers and the manufacturers in the industry.

The seminar was attended by 65 participants which included academics, media professionals, administrators, scholars and social activists.

Indore, 10-11 August 1996

Inaugurating the Seminar, the Vice-Chancellor, Devi Ahilya University, Prof. A. A. Abbasi said that contemporary media was being dominated by the elements inimical to the concerns of the society at large and it was, therefore, important that persons working in the media should try to safeguard the professional interests. Prof. Abbasi also stressed that the academic institutions imparting training and education in print and electronic journalism should improve their curriculum and make it relevant to the emerging needs of the society. Chairing the session on 'Media, Human Values and Ethics—Social Responsibility of Media', the Chairman of Utkarsha, Dr. P. N. Mishra said that journalism had been accepted as a means of service to the society in India, but because of the increasing pressure from the market forces many literary magazines have stopped their publication. He stressed that journalism should propagate social and ethical values.

Presiding over the plenary session on the concluding day, Justice R. D. Shukla said that the modern media was catering more to the needs of handful of market forces who were using it to create confusion among the masses. Justice Shukla said : Media is no more related to the ground realities of the society. It is true that the market forces are influencing the media and are deciding its direction but at the same time they also need media to survive in the competition. So, in a way, the media and market forces have become interdependent and in this new arrangement the interests of the people have taken a back seat.

Chairing the session on 'Media and Market Forces and Social Transformation', the Principal of Indore School of Social Work, Dr. W. S. K. Phillips emphasized that media in present day market forces was turning the present day society into an acquisition based society.

The seminar was attended by 55 participants including the faculty members from the Institute of Management Studies and Centre for Vocational Studies.

Shimla, 15-16 September 1996

The competition faced by the print media, not only from satellite television but also from electronic newspaper available through computers, was underlined by Mr. Kanwar Sandhu, Resident Editor of the *Indian Express* in his Keynote Address at the Seminar. He stressed the need for the newspaper industry to adopt new trends in order to adequately face challenges from audio-visual media. Elaborating the idea further, Mr. Sandhu said : In the emerging scenario, people would no longer be dependent on newspapers for news. A discernible influence of market forces was that the line dividing the editorial and advertisement sections was fast vanishing. Above all, the changing relationship between the editor and the proprietor was also likely to affect the newspapers. The arrangement to have proprietors as managing editors would work only if the persons concerned had good grounding in journalism. These challenges could be met by adopting a global approach and focus on indepth reporting and news analysis.

Inaugurating the seminar, Mr. Adarsh Sood, Mayor of the Shimla Municipal Corporation said : The satellite television invasion was having an adverse impact on the print media and it was high time that the newspaper industry took steps to face the growing challenge from the skies. In this era of commercialisation, newspapers must be made more attractive and informative so that they could continue to play an effective role in educating the society which was becoming increasingly addicted to the electronic media. Sometimes it appeared that because of the impact of market forces and consequences thereof, the media has contributed towards making India a consumers' paradise. In our race towards material acquisition we are throwing to winds our value-based culture and heritage. The result of free wheeling market of media, if allowed unchecked, will affect all possible aspects of the social milieu—cultural, educational as well as political.

The Organising Secretary of the Seminar, Dr. Vir Bala Aggarwal, from the Department of Journalism and Mass Communication, Himachal University, in her paper, Media and Market Forces—the Emerging Scenario said : Ethical choices have still to be made by media gate-keepers who shape the minds, attitudes and opinions of the people. Of late the concept being promoted is that selling newspapers is just like selling cakes of soap. The newspaper is a product and the emphasis is on packaging. The commercial and the business side, modern management methods and techniques, contract journalism, loss of authority of the editor to proprietor are some of the issues currently being confronted. A certain amount of conflict and social grievances were part of any growth-oriented society, and our media should not gloss over these social aspects of governance. She stressed the need for more concerted efforts, more research studies and advocacy groups to create a body of public opinion against the rapid onslaught of the commercialisation of media institutions in the country.

The Chairman of the Journalism Department, Mr. Vepa Rao said that the media also reflected the changing values of the society. He stressed institutional checks for journalism profession and lamented that dual-faced morality was becoming the order of the day. He strongly emphasised that the profession of journalism be licenced on the pattern of medical and law professions and the licence would remain valid till such time as the journalists adhere to the professional code of ethics.

In the concluding session of the seminar, opinion of the participants was elicited about the contemporary media scenario in the country. The participants were of the opinion that most of the T.V. programmes were alien to the Indian culture, and the influence of multi-national T.V. companies was growing on the programmes. They suggested that in order to improve the quality of media programmes, indiscriminate introduction of courses in journalism should be checked. The departments should properly be equipped with audio-visual aids. The Press Council of India should have state level media councils so that greater check could be enforced on the contents of newspapers.

Bombay, 5 October 1996

The one-day seminar offered an entirely different perspective on the impact of marketing forces on the working of the media. Whereas in other seminars, deep concern had been expressed on the onslaught of marketing forces on media, the participants in the seminar held in Bombay found that there was nothing wrong with marketing forces dominating the media. Presiding over the inaugural session of the seminar, the Senior Marketing Consultant, Mr. Ashok Aggarwal expressed his delight on these kinds of seminars being arranged in India, which would help create awareness among participants about the impact of marketing forces on media. He also mentioned about the invasion of satellite television in India. Twenty-seven cities in India were at present covered by satellites, software from foreign countries was being projected by the media without censorship, which is creating, at times negative impact on the minds of the consumers.

The noted film producer and director, Mr. Vinay Dhumale observed that the topic raised many questions : Whether media is really achieving important social goals? The answer is negative. He opined that the basic quest of all media owners today was to make money. The live film on war in Iraq was the best sold software. Attitude of revenge and violence was becoming popular. Media requires a self-check and control.

The AMIC Country Representative, Prof. V. S. Gupta said : Whatever may be the compulsions of catering to the interests of investors and advertisers, efforts to curb *junk journalism* through an emphasis on professionalisation, both in journalism training and through the organisations of journalists should continue. Increasing public awareness of the consequences of *junk journalism* may be the best route to a healthier information diet.

In the concluding session, Pt. Vinod Sharma, a pioneer in Radio Broadcasting, emphatically said that there was no media which could compete with Radio because of its portability, price and penetration power among rural audience.

The FES Media Advisor, Mr. Rajeshwar Dyal said that tremendous changes in media have taken place due to market forces. The newspaper proprietors often dominated the editor in formulating the policy. He expressed the view that development—the stated objective of Doordarshan, enshrined in its mandate was completely lost sight of. The seminar was organized in collaboration with the K. C. College of Management Studies, and coordinated by the AMIC India West Zone Representative, Mr. G. T. Balani.

NATIONAL COLLOQUIUM

IIC, New Delhi, 19-20 October 1996

The National Colloquium organised at the India International Centre, New Delhi on 19-20 October 1996 provided the fitting finals to the series of five regional seminars.

While chairing the inaugural session, the General Secretary of the National Media Centre, Mr. Upendra Vajpeyi said : Market forces have their own positive role to play in dissemination of information and social interaction. But the "part" should not become bigger than the "whole". The information based power structure emerging as the most potent factor in determining all other parameters, it may be suicidal to surrender the media to the market forces. Just as the size of the country did not deter the small number of British traders to capture it politically, the size and population of the country will not prevent the international information operators from overpowering any country without formally capturing it.

He deeply regretted that the widest and most effective media—the electronic media was engaged in titilating popular sensualities to save itself from being crowded out from the market. In a way, the State was becoming a victim of its own acts of omission and commission. To resolve the conflict between immediate gain and future uncertainty, the option was being exercised in favour of immediate gain derived from all sorts of commercials and programmes irrespective of their malignant influence on impressionable minds.

Speaking on the occasion, Mr. S.Y. Qureshi, a senior Central Government official, working in the Ministry of Human Resource Development, expressed his deep anguish at the indifference of media to the social responsibility. He also regretted that every discussion on media started and ended with television. There is certainly more to media than television. In Doordarshan public service broadcasting should be given proper priority. He was deeply distressed at the unhealthy social practices being encouraged by television by promoting products like PAN PARAG rather than launching a public service campaign in the aid of prevention of drug abuse, AIDS, etc.

The Resident Representative, Friedrich Ebert Stiftung, Dr. Horst Mund, in his opening statement, while appreciating the efforts of AMIC India in organising five Regional Seminars and said that the National Colloquium was being organised at a time when the media and communications scenario in India and other developing countries was changing at an accelerating speed, making the task of policy makers and media professionals a daunting one.

Entertainment and More Entertainment

Speaking on the issues of economic liberalisation and growing influence of market forces, Dr. Mund said that after the gulf war, satellite and cable television have grown at a tremendous speed all over Asia. In India besides the foreign satellite channels, large number of private channels in Hindi and several other regional languages have started their operations. For foreign channels, viewers in India are a prime target. Undoubtedly, these private satellite channels have started their operations purely from the commercial point of view. Since this business of running a private satellite channel requires very high capital investments all-out efforts are made to get as much commercial revenue as possible through advertising. Advertising revenues will grow and keep growing, only when viewership keeps growing, larger and larger. This is ensured by providing entertainment, more entertainment and more entertainment, 24 hours a day, 365 days a year. Undoubtedly, entertainment of viewers is also important. But so much of importance and all kinds of entertainment? *Clean and healthy entertainment programmes are certainly needed but showing of mind boggling programmes, alien to viewer's culture cannot be the only objective of a powerful medium like television in a developing country like India where several pressing issues need attention and continuous cooperation of media.*

Referring to the situation of television in Germany, Dr. Mund said : It seems that a division of labour between private and public channels could emerge in Germany where viewers switch to private channels for light entertainment and to the public television service for news, features and other programmes which contain a relatively high degree of information. Thus, there is even increasing pressure on private channels to improve the quality, particularly of their news services. He felt that similar positive developments might happen in television in India also.

Dr. Mund concluded by briefly touching upon the work of the Media and Communication Department in the International Cooperation Division of FES. He pointed out that FES's support is to benefit specially those who have remained underprivileged by existing structures—the economically weaker countries—to strengthen them; the poorer groups in society (e.g. rural people)—to improve their position in it; the trade unions as one of the FES's traditional target groups—to help them assert their demands.

Earlier, in his Introductory Remarks, the Country Representative, AMIC, Prof. V. S. Gupta said : The Colloquium would seek to focus attention on the changes and issues involved as a result of the impact of market forces on media, take note of the developing situation and suggest directions and initiatives for the media by having a congregation of academics, ad-professionals, media practitioners and NGOs who would like to explore future trends. He hoped that during the two days of intensive interaction, there would be ample opportunity to share our perceptions and evolve suitable strategy to combat the rapid onslaught of the market forces on the working of media.

In his message, the AMIC Secretary General, Mr. Vijay Menon said : AMIC has endeavoured to assist the region's media with conferences, seminars and workshops focusing on changing technologies and economies and by trying to impart the new skills that the new times require. In India, the encouragement and support of the New Delhi office of the Friedrich-Ebert-Stiftung (FES) have enabled AMIC India to organise workshops and seminars designed to stimulate debate and discussions on media issues of national concern; media and development, rural press, problems and prospects; national media policy and most recently, media and market forces. This is indeed a partnership for progress. It is our hope that this valuable support will continue in the years ahead to the benefit of communication practitioners, researchers and scholars and the media in the country.

The veteran journalist, Mr. N. S. Jagannathan chaired the session on 'Impact of Market Forces on Satellite and Cable Television Programmes' and 'Changing Role of Editor versus Advertising'.

In his presentation, Emergent Communication Technology and Commercial Pressures, Dr. Sunil Misra said : In the field of television transmission, all the available channels except Doordarshan to an extent have come to be dominated by monopolistic organisations for whom perhaps public service ranks lowest in order of priority. It is a well documented fact that when an alternative is available to the audiences in the form of high entertainment programmes, they would prefer to shift from the serious programmes. Thus, in order to attract greater number of viewers and thereby rake in profits from commercial advertisements, most of the channels are competing in presenting programmes which cater only to the popular tastes.

Dr. Misra pointed out that the state owned media appear to be joining the race for generating commercial revenue and asked : Can the government not provide financial support for Akashvani and Doordarshan to enable them pursue the basic roles and responsi-bilities as indicated in their motto of "*Satyam Shivam Sundaram*" and "*Bahujan Hitai-Bahujan Sukhai*", and should the two media continue to rely on commercial revenue for additional resource generation.

Making his presentation, the Director of Commonwealth Educational Media Centre for Asia, Mr. Gopal Saksena, regretted that the television, which was universally regarded as a serious business of ideas and creativity, had largely become a business of pure economics. The earlier concepts of its being a major source of education and information were no longer valid. Since survival of different channels had become dependent upon advertisement revenue, TV was shaping up primarily as a vehicle for entertainment. Mr. Saksena pointed out that the success of advertising depended on public confidence and nothing should be done which might impair this confidence. At the same time, advertising should not offend morality, decency, aesthetic perceptions and social susceptibilities of the people. The market forces will continue to have tremendous impact on our television. It is for those responsible for running a television or cable network to withstand this pressure.

While chairing the second session, Mr. Jagannathan pointed out that the newspaper editor had several foes and not just advertising. He had to face hundreds of pressures, both informal as well as formal. Market forces operate on press in various ways. Is reducing prices best way to compete? How about improving the quality of contents of newspapers and making them more commentative and analytical? Managerial and proprietor's pressures on editors were other aspects which needed discussion.

A senior journalist and media advisor to the Government of Jammu and Kashmir, Mr. Ram Mohan Rao pointed out that the very first Press Commission had tried to insulate editor from market forces and from the owners. The government issued directives to the effect. The editor was the final authority. In the first and second Press Commissions, efforts were also made to regulate as to how much space was to be devoted to advertisements and news/comments. Newspapers at that time were not run as commercial ventures. Newspapers were never able to earn costs by selling only. While bigger newspapers met 20 per cent of costs by sale, average was 40-48 per cent cost of newsprint plus services, rest of the income was through advertisements. If a newspaper depends on government advertisements and runs campaign against the government, it will not work.

Mr. Rao said : Of late, some changes are visible wherein the editors are given better pay packages and are employed on contractual basis. Advertising too which was a sort of open ended profession has become professional. Advertisers are now communicators. Since newspapers had to depend on money and take into account the role of advertising, the editor's role has naturally eroded in the process.

In his paper, Indian Identity in a Global Village—Media has to Reassert its Role; Mr. Gopal Mishra regretted that the market forces have overtaken the Indian media's role and the influence of the editor and the editorial team has shrunk considerably in the country's major newspapers. Painting a grim picture of the situation obtaining at present, Mr. Mishra said : Either professional editors have been sacked or they have run to other medium or business for their survival. Some of senior journalists who could not get appropriate opportunities in electronic and foreign media are pressurised to work as commercial managers and PR managers for the management not connected for the uplift of the profession. To certain extent for all this, we all are jointly responsible. While international media also play upon commercial stories yet care is taken to do it judiciously. The Indian press, however, in the last decade or so has crossed all limits to fulfil personal motives. This need of professionalism has forced and divided the journalists into two segments—one, who believe in professional ethics and unbiased reporting and second, those who have unhesitatingly adopted the role of an executive committed to push a certain product in the market. With the emerging market friendly atmosphere, the first victim is the editorial leadership, which has already partly succumbed to the product concept of a newspaper or a media outfit.

In the Open Discussion following points were made :

— Distinction between advertising and editorial requirements is getting blurred;
— Institution of editor is getting eroded. Production cost of newspapers has increased and the management/ circulation has become the main criterion. Salesmanship gets priority over editorial inputs;
— Pages have been increasing for advertisements and there is staleness of news. Economic contents of newspapers

are increasing at the cost of hard news;

— Newspapers are completely dominated by corporate sector. Editors are working at the whims and fancies of proprietors; and
— Market forces are corrupting journalists. There is a need to redefine the role of journalists.

While chairing the session, Influence of Advertising on Media Structures, Mr. D. K. Bose, Executive Director, R. K. Swamy Advertising said : The last five years have witnessed newspapers go through major changes in widening the readership base. The major changes introduced are colour, special pull outs and supplements, more editions, local editions, etc. The magazines on the other hand have either killed commercially unviable titles or have introduced special interest titles. Radio has been given a new life with the introduction of FM channels, attracting specific and select audience groups. TV is in the midst of a revolution. Over 50 channels, both national and regional, many of them telecasting 24 hours a day are now available through terrestrial, satellite and cable.

Defining the impact of advertising on media, Mr. Bose added that the dependence on advertising had increased. Internally, the marketing department exercised greater influence on editorial policy, whereas externally, the demands of advertisers to share editorial space have increased. In his concluding remarks he added that when economic structure underwent a change, it led to socio-economic changes throwing out old patterns and bringing in new ones. It was, therefore, important that media acted as a gatekeeper and did not buckle under pressure.

In his paper, Advertising and Market-driven Journalism, Prof. Gupta pointed out that as early as 1985 the Working Group on Software Planning for Doordarshan (Joshi Committee Report) stressed the need to prevent '*the appropriation of television by the emerging forces of commercialism and consumerism*'. However, advertising seems to have taken over the television industry. Big money and bigger target audience, commercial extravaganza and glitzy advertisements dominate television programming. He referred to the Sengupta Committee Report on Prasar Bharati which had said : *In the wake of large influx of alien entertainment, directed to the top crust, the minority with growing purchasing power and propensity to spend, the significance of public service broadcasting needs no over-emphasis.* The high presence of more frothy entertainment, fun and frolic can only amuse for a while but cannot meet the real desires of people unless the fare offered is imbued with social purpose.

He referred in detail to a recent publication '*Market-driven Journalism : Let the Citizen Beware?*', by a former newspaper reporter and researcher, Mr. John H. McManus, who has written : Executive editors throughout the country are being trained not to select news of interest to their community as a whole, but only for those people who live in selective neighbourhoods that has certain characteristics wanted by major advertisers. The practice of selecting news in order to make advertising more effective is becoming so common that it has achieved the status of *scientific procedure*.

Prof. Gupta concluded : Whatever may be the compulsions of catering to the interests of investors and advertisers, efforts to curb *junk journalism* through an emphasis on professionalisation, both in journalism training and in organisation of reporters and editors, should continue.

In her paper, Market-driven Media, media analyst, Ms. Nandini Prasad said : In its race to sustain and subsequently keep on increasing its viewership, Doordarshan has fallen a prey to market-driven TV situation and seems to be quite satisfied with its success in earning more and more commercial revenue. A public service broadcasting channel is no different from private channels whose sole aim is to maximise their profits. As such, all TV channels including Doordarshan are governed by the forces of demand (of their viewers) and supply (of entertainment programmes). Now, can a country like India afford the use of the most powerful medium like TV only for entertainment purposes?

Referring to the role of government, Ms. Prasad said : It seems that the government has given tacit approval to the market forces governing the media. First it introduced economic liberalisation inviting multinationals and foreign investors, not only in the core sectors but also in the consumer products area. Obviously the investors will seek the help of media for promoting their products through intensive advertising. And, therefore, the media contents are dictated by the advertisements. She concluded that while the media owners, practitioners and investors in the private sector may be guided by the profit motive, public service broadcasting networks of Doordarshan and All India Radio should try to achieve the objectives of a welfare state.

Chairing the concluding session, Emerging Market Forces and Social Responsibility of Media, Mr. Ajit Bhattacharjea, Director, Press Institute of India, expressed his apprehension regarding the play of market forces and their impact on print media. He lamented nostalgically about the loss of the supremacy of the Press as an Institution. Hailing as he does from the print medium, it was not difficult to understand his predicament.

At the outset he felt that the entertainment component and sex and violence predominated the media. In the case of TV there cannot be safeguard as it reaches into people's homes, their bedrooms and drawing rooms, and it is virtually impossible to shield the children from the influence. He felt that the real impact of this influence on tender and impressionable minds would be realised in the long run as the effect of TV advertising was very insidious and gradual on the minds of vulnerable sections and capable of brain washing them to change beliefs, value systems and lifestyles.

In the end he impressed upon the participants to think of ways to protect the viewers/readers from the negative impact of the market forces. The government has failed and therefore cannot be expected to do much, but the onus was on the media persons themselves to overcome this critical period. He suggested the constitution of an Independent Commission comprising eminent professionals, social scientists, psychologists, etc. to act as a watchdog.

Making his presentation on Emerging Market Forces and Social Responsibility of Media, Prof. Devesh Kishore, Head, EMPC, IGNOU, quoted the example of Turkey where the media provided free health awareness slots. In our own country laudable work was being done by the Zee Channel in providing computer and management education through the medium. He espoused the cause of Radio as a cost effective medium, ideally suited to this country, which remains unexploited so far and cited the successful launch of the FM Radio for local broadcasting in metros. Interactive and participatory use of video technology has been tried in distance education with certain degree of success. It has been tried in development projects, such as the one in Pune to record the problems faced by farmers which were sent to the officials at the district and state level. Such feedback systems, with minimum loss of time, content and quality is found to be cost effective and feasible too. Prof. Kishore was of the opinion that the market forces were here to stay and it made practical sense to follow the consumer's trend and exploit it best in the interest of the society at large.

In his presentation, Social Responsibility of Media for Rural Development, Dr. B. S. Hansra, Asstt. Director General, ICAR, referred to the studies conducted on communication effectiveness which proved that Radio as a medium had provided greater impact in agricultural communication. As much as nine hours a week on Radio were devoted for this during the Green Revolution. This against one plus one (two hours) for Agriculture and Rural Development was considerably a very small allocation on state channels, he said. The print scenario was even more dismal. It was virtually nil in the national dailies, not particularly relevant in the vernacular dailies which have just begun to devote a special page for this in the recent past. He urged for greater quantum of coverage in the media for this vital sector.

A senior journalist and former editor of *Dainik Tribune*, Mr. Radhey Shyam Sharma said that new trends and policies and even the media have affected the mindset and lifestyle of the people. Consequently agricultural and rural news were reflected more and more in the regional press. The information explosion has broadened the mindset and there was a greater stress on economic value. Everything had become a business and a saleable commodity including education and health and privatization of public services was being considered widely.

A social activist, Ms. Indra Bishnoi intervened to stress the urgent need to highlight national issues and appropriate social values through media.

She said that except for Krishi Darshan, Doordarshan had no other programme for the farmers and rural women, whereas there was greater need to inform and educate the rural farmers and farm women on the social issues and rural development programmes. She expected that the government should strive to bring Doordarshan out of the clutches of commercialisation.

A Communication Expert from Australia, Ms. Melisa

Butcher suggested strategies such as introduction of licence fees, subsidies, niche marketing, community radio with no profit motive, for meeting the resource crunch. She shared the experience of a small village in Nepal with local cable TV and around 200 clients catering to local programming. She said that one can exist with commercial TV better that way.

The FES Media Advisor, Mr. Rajeshwar Dyal, in the final sum up of the series of five regional seminars and the National Colloquium, wherein over 500 participants had taken part and around 75 papers were presented, congratulated the AMIC India team headed by Prof. V. S. Gupta for undertaking this mammoth task systematically. He was quite appreciative of the pace of these seminars, considering the fact that the Steering Committee had been constituted only a few months ago. The seminars held in Hyderabad, Patna, Indore, Shimla and Bombay had drawn representatives from different sections of the media in the country. The views expressed by and large reflected the impact of market forces at that level and together can be reflective of the national perspective.

ANNEXURES

ANNEXURE I

CODE OF ADVERTISING PRACTICE OF THE ADVERTISING STANDARDS COUNCIL OF INDIA

CHAPTER - I

To Ensure the Truthfulness and Honesty of Representations and Claims Made by Advertisements and to Safeguard against Misleading Advertisements.

1. Advertisements must be truthful. All descriptions, claims and comparisons which relate to matters of objectively ascertainable fact should be capable of substantiation. Advertisers and advertising agencies are required to produce such substantiation as and when called upon to do so by The Advertising Standards Council of India.
2. Where advertising claims are expressly stated to be based on or supported by independent research or assessment, the source and date of this should be indicated in the advertisement.
3. Advertisements should not contain any reference to any person, firm or institution without due permission; nor should a picture of any generally identifiable person be used in advertising without due permission.
4. Advertisements shall not distort facts nor mislead the consumer by means of implications or omissions. Advertisements shall not contain statements or visual presentations which directly or by implication or by omission or by ambiguity or by exaggeration are likely to mislead the consumer about the product advertised or the advertiser or about any other product or advertiser.
5. Advertisements shall not be so framed as to abuse the trust of consumers or exploit their lack of experience or knowledge. No advertisement shall be permitted to contain any claim so exaggerated as to lead to grave or

widespread disappointment in the minds of consumers. For example :

(a) Products shall not be described as 'free' where there is any direct cost to the consumer other than the actual cost of any delivery, freight or postage. Where such costs are payable by the consumer a clear statement that this is the case shall be made in the advertisement.

(b) Where a claim is made that if one product is purchased another product will be provided 'free', the advertiser is required to show as and when called upon by The Advertising Standards Council of India that the price paid by the consumer for the product which is offered for purchase with the advertised incentive is no more than the prevalent price of the product without the advertised incentive.

(c) Claims which use expressions such as 'Up to five years' guarantee' or 'Prices from as low as Y' are not acceptable if there is a likelihood of the consumer being misled either as to the extent of the availability or as to the applicability of the benefits offered.

(d) Special care and restraint has to be exercised in advertisements addressed to those suffering from weakness, any real or perceived inadequacy of any physical attributes such as height or bust development, obesity, illness, impotence, infertility, baldness and the like to ensure that claims or representations, directly or by implication, do not exceed what is considered prudent by generally accepted standards or medical practice and the actual efficacy of the product.

(e) Advertisements inviting the public to invest money shall not contain statements which may mislead the consumer in respect of the security offered, rates of return or terms of amortization : where any of the fore-going elements are contingent upon the continuance of or change in existing conditions, or any other assumptions, such conditions or assumptions must be clearly indicated in the advertisements.

(f) Advertisements inviting the public to take part in lotteries of prize competitions permitted under the law or which hold out the prospects of gifts shall state clearly all material conditions so as to enable the consumers to obtain a true and fair view of their prospects in such activity. Further, such advertiser shall make adequate provisions for the judging of such competitions, announcement of the results and the fair distribution of prizes or gifts according to the advertised terms and conditions within a reasonable period of time. With regard to the announcement of results, it is clarified that the advertiser's responsibility under this section of the Code is discharged adequately if the advertiser publicizes the main result in the media used to announce the competition as far as is practicable, and advises the individual winners by post.

6. Obvious untruths or exaggerations intended to amuse or to catch the eye of the consumer are permissible, provided that they are clearly to be seen as humorous or hyperbolic and not likely to be understood as making literal or misleading claims for the advertised product.

CHAPTER - II

To Ensure that Advertisements are not Offensive to Generally Accepted Standards of Public Decency.

Advertisements should contain nothing indecent, vulgar or repulsive which is likely, in the light of generally prevailing standards of decency and propriety, to cause grave or widespread offence.

CHAPTER - III

To Safeguard against the Indiscriminate Use of Advertising in Situations or for the Promotion of Products which are Regarded as Hazardous to Society or to Individuals to a degree or of a type which is Unacceptable to Society at Large.

1. No advertisement shall be permitted which :

   (a) Tends to incite people to crime or to promote disorder and violence or intolerance.
   (b) Derides any race, caste, colour, creed or nationality.
   (c) Presents criminality as desirable or directly or indirectly encourages people—particularly children—to emulate it or conveys the *modus operandi* of any crime.
   (d) Adversely affects friendly relations with a foreign State.

2. Advertisements addressed to children shall not contain anything, whether in illustration or otherwise, which might result in their physical, mental or moral harm or which exploits their vulnerability. For example, no advertisement :

   (a) Shall encourage children to enter strange places or to converse with strangers in an effort to collect coupons, wrappers, labels or the like.
   (b) Should depict children leaning dangerously outside windows, over bridges or climbing dangerous cliffs and the like.
   (c) Should show children climbing or reaching dangerously to reach products or for any other purpose.
   (d) Should show children using or playing with matches or any inflammable or explosive substance; or playing with or using sharp knives, guns or mechanical or electrical appliances, the careless use of which could lead to their suffering cuts, burns, shocks or other injury.
   (e) Shall feature minors for tobacco or alcohol based products.

3. Advertisements shall not, without justifiable reason, show or refer to dangerous practices or manifest a disregard for safety or encourage negligence.
4. Advertisements should contain nothing which is in breach of the law, or omit anything which the law requires.

5. Advertisements shall not propagate products, the use of which is banned under the law.

CHAPTER - IV

To Ensure that Advertisements Observe Fairness in Competition such that the Consumer's Need to be Informed on Choices in the Market-place and the Canons of Generally Accepted Competitive Behaviour in Business are both Served.

1. Advertisements containing comparisons with other manufacturers or suppliers or with other products, including those where a competitor is named, are permissible in the interests of vigorous competition and public enlightenment, provided :

   (a) It is clear what aspects of the advertiser's product are being compared with what aspects of the competitor's product.
   (b) The subject matter of comparison is not chosen in such a way as to confer an artificial advantage upon the advertiser or so as to suggest that a better bargain is offered than is truly the case.
   (c) The comparisons are factual, accurate and capable of substantiation.
   (d) There is no likelihood of the consumer being misled as a result of the comparison, whether about the product advertised or that with which it is compared.
   (e) The advertisement does not unfairly denigrate, attack or discredit other products, advertisers or advertisements directly or by implication.

2. Advertisements shall not make unjustifiable use of the name or initials of any other firm, company or institution, nor take unfair advantage of the goodwill attached to the trade mark or symbol of another firm or its product or the goodwill acquired by its advertising campaign.
3. Advertisements shall not be so similar to other advertisements in general layout, copy, slogans, visual presentations, music or sound effects as to be likely to mislead or confuse consumers.

ANNEXURE II

THE CODE FOR COMMERCIAL ADVERTISING ON ALL INDIA RADIO

Code for Commercial Advertising over Radio and Television

Definition— In this Code, unless the context otherwise requires—

(i) The term "Sponsored Programme" means any programme material which is planned, produced and/or paid for by an organization or individual, to be called 'the sponsor' for the purpose of being broadcast/telecast over sound radio or television in India.

(ii) "Director General" means, the Director General, All India Radio, or any officer duly authorized by him on his behalf and includes the Director, Television Centre.

(iii) "Sponsor" means any individual or organization including a commercial concern who has offered a programme for broadcast/telecast over the radio or television.

(iv) "Spot Advertisement" means any direct advertisement mentioning products, their merits, prices and other related details.

(v) "Advertiser" means any individual or organization including a commercial concern which has offered an advertisement for broadcast/telecast over the radio or television.

(vi) "Advertisement" includes any item of publicity inserted in the programmes broadcast by the competent authority in consideration of payment to All India Radio.

Scope

(a) A sponsored programme shall constitute a substantive

Note : All references to television in this Code should be ignored as a new Code for Commercial Advertising on Doordarshan has been promulgated as Annexure III.

broadcast/telecast programme, as distinct from material which directly advertises any specific wares or goods or products. The name of the sponsor shall be broadcast immediately before and after the sponsored programme.

(b) The Director General, All India Radio, shall be the sole judge of the suitability or otherwise of a sponsored programme for broadcast and his decision in this regard shall be final.

(c) Broadcast time shall be sold to the sponsor at the sole discretion of the Director General, All India Radio, according to the prescribed rates.

(d) To ensure acceptable programme and technical quality of the sponsored programme, the Director General, All India Radio, may require the sponsor to undertake an adequate number of rehearsals of the said material in the studios of All India Radio, to the satisfaction of the Director General or his representative. The time so utilized by the sponsor shall be paid for by him separately, according to rates prescribed for the purpose.

(e) Advertising must be clearly distinguishable from news content in news programmes.

(f) The word 'guarantee' in respect of the advertised goods should be used with caution and sparingly and only in relation to some specific description or quality and the detailed terms of any such guarantee must be available for inspection by All India Radio. Where the guarantee is associated with an offer to return the purchase price, it must be made quite clear to what it applies and in what way it protects the purchaser.

I. Introduction

Advertising is an important and legitimate means for the seller to awaken interest in his goods and services. The success of advertising depends on public confidence; hence no practice should be permitted which tends to impair this confidence.

The following standards of conduct are laid down in order to counteract the misuse of advertising and to promote further development of the sense of responsibility on the part of advertisers to the consumer.

Responsibility for the observance of these rules rests with :

(a) The advertiser on whose account the advertisement is issued.
(b) The advertiser or the advertising agent who has created the advertisement.

All those engaged in advertising are strongly recommended to familiarize themselves with the legislation affecting advertising in this country, particularly the following Acts and the rules framed under them :

1. Drugs and Cosmetics Act, 1940.
2. Drugs Control Act, 1950.
3. Drugs and Magic Remedies (Objectionable Advertisements) Act, 1954.
4. Copyright Act, 1957.
5. Trade and Merchandise Marks Act, 1958.
6. Prevention of Food Adulteration Act, 1954.
7. Pharmacy Act, 1948.
8. Prize Competition Act, 1955.
9. Emblems and Names (Prevention of Improper Use) Act, 1950.

The Code

II. General Rules of Conduct in Advertising

1. Advertising should be so designed as to conform to the laws of the country and should not offend against morality, decency and religious susceptibilities of the people.
2. No advertisement should be permitted :

   (i) which derides any race, caste, colour, creed, nationality except wherein such usage would be for the specific purpose of effective dramatization, such as combating prejudice;
   (ii) which is against any of the objectives, principles, or provisions of the Constitution of India;
   (iii) which will tend to incite people to crime or to

promote disorder, violence or breach of law;

(iv) which presents criminality as desirable or furnish details of crime or imitation thereof;

(v) which would adversely affect friendly relations with foreign States;

(vi) which exploits the national emblems, or any part of the Constitution, or the person or personality or national leader or state dignitary;

3. In all other respects, the Director General, All India Radio, will be guided for purposes of commercial broadcasting and telecasting in All India Radio by the Code of Ethics for Advertising in India issued by the Advertising Council of India (relevant excerpts appended), as modified from time to time.

4. Notwithstanding anything contained herein, this Code is subject to such modifications/directions as may be made/issued by the Government of India from time to time.

III. Procedure for the Enforcement of the Code

(a) All complaints or reports on contraventions of the Code, received by All India Radio shall be in the first instance referred by Director General, All India Radio, to the Advertisers' Association(s) concerned, who should be requested to take suitable action.

(b) Members of member associations having complaints under the Code against members of other member association(s) should, in the first instance, address their complaint to the member association(s) concerned.

(c) If complaints under the Code cannot be satisfactorily resolved at member association(s) level, they should be reported to All India Radio which will consider suitable action.

(d) For any complaints under the Code received by All India Radio, concerning an offending party outside the purview of the various member association(s), All India Radio itself will draw attention of the offending party to the contravention and consider suitable action.

(e) The sponsor shall undertake to indemnify All India

Radio against any legal claim that may be brought against it as a result of the broadcast of a sponsored programme or any portion thereof.

Excerpts from the Code of Ethics for Advertising in India Issued by the Advertising Council of India

Introduction

Along with the development of a very complex distribution system, the requirements of a market economy, faced with the need for ensuring a regular flow of mass production, have given rise to the development of new techniques of sales promotion.

Of these, advertising has proved itself to be of inestimable value for producers and distributors as well as for consumers. It enables the former to maintain contact with customers who are widely scattered and often unknown, and it assists the latter in choosing those goods and services that are the best suited to their particular requirements.

Advertising has become an important social and economic force in the world of today. It is, therefore, essential that any unfair advertising practice likely to alienate public confidence should be eliminated. Hence the need for rules of conduct drawn up for the purpose of preventing possible abuses and of promoting an increasing sense of responsibility towards the consumer on the part of the advertisers, advertising agencies and media owners and suppliers.

Recognizing that the legitimate function of advertising is the advocacy of the merits of particular products or services this code is intended to be applied in the spirit as well as in the letter and should be taken to set out the minimum standards to be observed by the parties concerned. This Code does override all ethical standards in advertising laid down by individual organizations, but it does not supersede the standards of practice laid down by individual organizations as incumbent upon their own members and applying to their own particular trade or industry.

General Rules of Conduct in Advertising

1. Advertising should be so designed as to conform not only

to the laws but also to the moral, aesthetic and religious sentiments of the country in which it is published.

2. No advertisement likely to bring advertising into contempt or disrepute should be permitted. Advertising should not take advantage of the superstition or ignorance of the general public.
3. No advertisements of talismans, charms and character reading from photographs or such other matter as will trade on the superstition of the general public shall be permitted.
4. Advertising should be truthful, avoid distorting facts and misleading the public by means of implications and omissions. For instance, it should not mislead the consumer by false statements as to :

   (a) the character of the merchandise, i.e., its utility, materials, ingredients, origin, etc.
   (b) the price of the merchandise, its value, its suitability or terms of purchase.
   (c) the services accompanying purchase, including delivery, exchange, return, repair, upkeep, etc.
   (d) personal recommendations of the article or service. Testimonials which are fictitious and/or fraudulent or the originals of which cannot be produced must not be used. Anyone using testimonials in advertisements is as responsible for the statements made in them as he would be if he had made them himself.
   (e) the quality of the value of competing goods or the trustworthiness of statements made by others.

5. No advertisement should be permitted to contain any claim so exaggerated as to lead inevitably to disappointment in the mind of the public. Special care is called for the following cases :

   (a) Advertisement addressed to those suffering from illness. (In this respect the Code of Standards of Advertising in relation to medicine must be adhered to.)
   (b) Advertisements inviting the public to invest money. Such advertisements should not contain statements

which may mislead the public in respect of the security offered, rates of return, or terms of amortization.

(c) Advertisements inviting the public to take part in lotteries or competitions such as are permitted by law or which hold out the prospect of gifts. Such advertisements should state clearly all the conditions for the lottery or competition or the conditions for the distribution of the gifts.

(d) The publication of employment notices requiring fees for application forms, prospectus, etc. and security deposits should be forbidden except when such advertisements emanate from Governmental or quasi-Governmental sources.

6. Methods of advertising designed to create confusion in the mind of the consumer as between goods by one maker and another maker are unfair and should not be used. Such methods may consist in :

   (a) the imitation of the trademark or name of competitor or the packaging or labelling of goods; or
   (b) the imitations of advertising devices, copy, layouts or slogans.

7. Advertising should endeavour to gain the goodwill of the public on the basis of the merits of the goods or services advertised. Direct comparison with competing goods or firms and disparaging references are in no circumstances permitted.
8. Indecent, vulgar, suggestive, repulsive or offensive themes or treatment should be avoided in all advertisements. This also applies to such advertisements which in themselves are not objectionable as defined above, but which advertise objectionable books, photographs or other matter and thereby lead to their sale and circulation.
9. No advertisement should offer to refund money paid.
10. The use of National Emblems is prohibited by law in advertisements, trademarks, etc., except by Governments or Governmental agencies. Also the use of the picture of

Mahatma Gandhi, the President, the Vice-President and the Prime Minister of India is forbidden in such advertisements, trademarks, etc., except by previous permission. This rule does not apply to advertising of books, films or other items in which these personages form the chief subject.

Code of Standards in Relation to the Advertising of Medicines and Treatments

This Code has been drafted for the guidance of advertisers, manufacturers, distributors, advertising agents, publishers and suppliers of various advertising media. The harm to the individual that may result from exaggerated, misleading or unwarranted claims justifies the adoption of a very high standard and the inclusion of considerable detail in a Code to guide those who are concerned with this form of advertising.

Newspaper and other advertising media are urged not to accept advertisements in respect of any product or treatment from any advertiser or advertising agent who disregards the provisions of this Code in any form of advertising or publicity relating to that product or treatment.

The provisions of this Code do not apply to an advertisement published by or under the authority of a Government, Ministry or Department, nor to an advertisement published only in journals circulated to Registered Medical Practitioners, Registered Dentists, Registered Pharmacists or Registered Nurses.

Section I

General Principles

1. *Cure* : No advertisement should contain a claim to cure any ailment of symptoms of ill-health, nor should an advertisement contain a word of expression used in such a form or context as to mean in the positive sense the extirpation of any ailment, illness or disease.
2. *Illness etc. properly requiring medical attention* : No advertisement should contain any matter which can be regarded as an offer of medicine or product for, or advice

relating to, the treatment of serious diseases, complaints, conditions, indications or symptoms which should rightly receive the attention of a registered medical practitioner (See Sec. 2).

3. *Misleading or exaggerated claims* : No advertisement should contain any matter which directly or by implication misleads or departs from the truth as to the composition, character or action of the medicine or treatment advertised or as to its suitability for the purpose for which it is recommended.
4. *Appeals to fear* : No advertisement should be calculated to induce fear on the part of the reader that he is suffering, or may without treatment suffer from an ailment, illness or disease.
5. *Diagnosis or treatment by correspondence* : No advertisement should offer to diagnose by correspondence diseases, conditions or any symptoms of ill-health in a human being or request from any person or a statement of his or any other person's symptoms of ill-health with a view to advertising as to or providing for treatment of such conditions of ill-health by correspondence. Nor should any advertisement offer to treat by correspondence any ailment, illness, disease, or svmptoms thereof in a human being.
6. *Disparaging references*: No advertisement should directly or by implication disparage the products, medicines or treatments of another advertiser or manufacturer or registered medical practitioner or the medical profession.
7. *College, clinic, institute, laboratory* : No advertisement should contain these or similar terms unless an establishment corresponding with the description used does in fact exist.
8. *Doctors, hospitals, etc.* : No advertisement should contain any reference to doctors or hospitals, whether Indian or foreign, unless such reference can be substantiated by independent evidence and can properly be used in the manner proposed.
9. *Products offered particularly to women* : No advertisement of products, medicines or treatments of disorders or irregularities peculiar to women should contain expres-

sions which may imply that the product, medicine or treatment advertised can be effective in inducing miscarriage.

10. *Family planning* : Advertisements for measures or apparatus concerning family planning would be permissible in so far as they conform to the generally accepted national policy in this behalf.
11. *Illustrations* : No advertisement should contain any illustration which by itself or in combination with words used in connection therewith is likely to convey a misleading impression, or if the reasonable inference to be drawn from such advertisement infringes any of the provisions of this Code.
12. *Exaggerated copy* : No advertisement should contain copy which is exaggerated by reason of improper use of words, phrases or methods of presentation, e.g., the use of the words "magic, magical, miracle, miraculous".
13. *Natural remedies* : No advertisement should claim or suggest contrary to the fact, that the article advertised is in the form in which it occurs in nature or that its value lies in its being a "natural" product.
14. *Special claims* : No advertisement should contain any reference which is calculated to lead the public to assume that the article, product, medicine or treatment advertised has some special property or quality which is in fact unknown or unrecognized.
15. *Sexual weakness, premature ageing, loss of virility* : No advertisement should claim that the product, medicine, or treatment advertised will promote sexual virility or be effective in treating sexual weakness or habits associated with sexual excess or indulgence or any ailment, illness or diseases associated with those habits.

    In particular, such terms as "premature ageing", "loss of virility", will be regarded as conditions for which medicines, products, appliances or treatment may not be advertised.
16. *Slimming, weight reduction or limitation or figure control* : No advertisement should offer any medical product for the purpose of slimming, weight reduction or limitation or figure control. Medical products intended to

reduce appetite will usually be regarded as being for slimming purposes.

17. *Tonics* : The use of this expression in advertisements should not imply that the product or medicine can be used in the treatment of sexual weakness.
18. *Hypnosis* : No advertisement should contain any offer to diagnose or treat complaints or conditions by hypnosis.
19. *Materials to students* : Materials meant for distribution in educational institutions must not carry advertisements of things other than those of value to students.

Section 2

Restrictions Imposed by Statute on Advertising of Medicines and Treatments

Rule 106 of the Drug Rules, 1945, provides that :

1. No drug may purport or claim to prevent or cure or may convey to the intending user thereof any idea that it may prevent or cure, one or more of the diseases or ailments specified in Schedule "J".

SCHEDULE J

Blindness	Bright's Disease	Cancer
Cataract	Deafness	Delayed Menstruation
Diabetes	Epilepsy	Hydrocele
Infantile Paralysis	Leprosy	Leucoderma
Lockjaw	Locomotor Ataxia	Insanity
Tuberculosis	Tumors	Venereal Diseases (in general)
Female Diseases (in general)	Fevers (in general)	Fits
Glaucoma	Goitre Soft Cancer	Gonorrhea
Heart Diseases	High Blood Pressure	Lupus
Obesity	Paralysis	Plague
Rupture	Sexual Impotence	Small Pox

2. No drug may purport to claim to procure or assist to procure, or may convey to the intending user thereof any idea that it may procure or assist to procure miscarriage in women.

Definition

"Drug" includes for internal or external use for human beings or animals all substances intended to be used for or in the treatment, mitigation, or prevention of disease in human beings or animals, other than medicines and substances exclusively used or prepared for use in accordance with the Ayurvedic or Unani system of medicines.

Standards of Practice for Radio Advertising

1. Because of the obligation of the broadcasting stations to their audience, it is necessary that meticulous supervision should be exercised over all programmes or sessions.

   The following rules should apply to all broadcasts, but particularly to broadcasts addressed to children :

   (a) All scripts must be carefully written having in mind the particular audience for which they are intended.
   (b) People should be encouraged in the art of correct speech and pronunciation. The use of slang and incorrect language should be discouraged.
   (c) All stories must reflect respect for law and order, adult authority, good morals and clean living.
   (d) Adventure stories may be accepted subject to the following prohibitions :

   No torture or suggestion of torture.
   No horror—present or impending.
   No use of supernatural or of superstition likely to arouse fear.
   No profanity or vulgarity.

   In order that people will not be emotionally upset, no programme or episode shall end with an incident which will create in their minds morbit suspense or hysteria.

(e) The themes of stories broadcast in all sessions should reflect fair play and considerate behaviour for one's fellow being. In particular, they should not undermine parental authority or the authority of teachers.

(f) As distinct from the collective aspects of children's programmes, it is suggested that sessions calculated to develop the tastes of individual children be arranged e.g. broadcast devoted to particular hobbies.

(g) No appeal should be made to the audience to help characters in the story by sending in box-tops or wrappers, nor may any actor remain in character and, in the commercial copy, address the individual urging him to purchase the product in order to keep the programme on the air, or make similar, appeals.

2. Commercial stations are bound not to accept any script continuity or programme matter for broadcasting, recorded or otherwise, which introduces or incorporates :

(a) Obscene and off-colour jokes or songs, oaths, sacrilegious expressions, anything of doubtful propriety.

(b) Statements or suggestions that may be considered offensive or religious views, racial traits and the like.

(c) Any statement that comments upon, ridicules or incorporates the name of any person in a derogatory manner or in relation to advertising.

(d) Matter of such nature as would destroy or tend to destroy public confidence or create any feeling of insecurity in the community.

3. Any such effects which might startle the listening public or in any manner is objectionable must not be incorporated in commercial announcements.

For example, and without limiting the scope, the use of the following sound effects will not be permitted in commercial announcements.

Rapid gunfire or rifle shots Screams
Sirens Racuous laughter and the like;
Bombardments Fire engines; Ambulance and Explosives.

4. Any pretence in advertising copy must be avoided and such copy shall not be accepted by commercial stations.
   "Dramatized testimonials" should not be incorporated in commercial announcements.
   "The simulation" of voices of a personality in connection with advertisements for commercial products is also prohibited unless bonafide evidence is available that such personality has given permission for the simulation of his or her voice and it is clearly understood that stations broadcasting such announcements are indemnified by the advertiser or advertising agency against any possible legal action.
5. No advertisement shall contain any matter which could be regarded as holding out for the prevention, cure or relief of serious diseases which should rightly be under the cure of a medical practitioner.
6. No broadcasting for any product will be permitted which describes graphically or repellently any internal bodily functions or matters which are generally not considered acceptable topics of conversation in social groups.
7. Special attention shall be paid to advertisements, relating to laxatives and other medicines with a view to exclusion of any distasteful statements. Comments as to the effects of medicine or medical treatment on specific organs of the body or in relation to any ailment or disease are also forbidden.

Standards of Practice for Advertising Agencies

(As approved by the Advertising Agencies Association of India, Bombay.)

1. Every member of the Association shall carry on his profession and business in such a manner as to uphold

the dignity and interests of the Association.

2. Every member shall refrain from canvassing Advertisers or prospective Advertisers in such a way as to reflect detrimentally upon Advertising Agents as a whole or this Association or any Advertising Agent in particular.
3. Canvassing is permitted subject to the condition that a member may make known to the client of another member its own capabilities as an Advertising Agency but may not submit a specific report or detailed recommendations concerning the client's advertising unless so requested by him in writing.
4. No member shall pay or undertake to pay or allow to an advertiser or his agent or representative, the whole or any portion of the standard rate of commission resulting or to result to such member from any advertising medium nor promise or procure or undertake to procure advertising space or facilities free of charge, to any advertiser, or at a reduced rate, nor supply or partly free to any advertiser, any advertising material, including finished drawings, or other art work, photography, blocks, stereos, matrices or the like, type-setting or printing nor defray in whole or in part the salary of an employee of an advertiser, nor grant any allowance, discount or the like nor render any service having the effect of rebating the commission allowed by an advertising medium. The sharing of commission with a member or overseas agency, or with another advertising agent recognized as an advertising agent by this Association shall, however, be permitted.
5. The practice of submitting speculative campaigns is unhealthy to the growth of the advertising services and that no speculative campaign shall be submitted by any member of the Advertising Agencies Association of India.

   By speculative campaign, it is meant, producing a campaign unsolicited by an advertiser and equally producing a campaign where the advertiser had requested one or more advertising agencies to do so, unaccompanied by a firm offer of business. That members shall notify the Secretary of the Association if any such queries were made by prospective advertiser, and that such information shall be circulated by the Secretary to all members.

6. Any member relinquishing an Account on the ground of slow payment, doubtful credit or incurring a bad debt, shall immediately notify the Secretary of the Association and such information shall be circulated in strictest confidence for information and protection of other members.
7. No business shall be accepted which is conditional upon the payment of commission or fee or reward to a third party not a full-time employee of the member either for introducing the business or for services in connection with the account thereafter. This rule, however, shall not preclude a member from employing copy-writers or production men at fees commensurate with the values of their work.

Obligations to Clients

1. Member Agencies must continue to render full agency service in reasonable conformity to the Association's Agency Service Standards.
2. Members shall retain either commission granted by Media owners or charge the clients a service fee which shall never be less than 15 per cent of the client's gross expenditure. Nor shall they supply material for advertising on any basis that can be considered as direct or indirect or secret rebating. Where no commission is allowed by the Media owner, the member will charge his clients a minimum of 15 per cent on the gross cost.
3. Members will not accept discounts or commission, other than the regular agency commission allowed by publishers without the client's knowledge and consent.
4. Members shall at all times use their best efforts to obtain for their clients the lowest rates to which such clients are entitled.

Obligations to Suppliers

Members shall take all steps to assure themselves as to the financial soundness of their clients.

Obligations to Fellow Agencies

1. Members are required to use fair methods of competition; not to offer the services enumerated above or services in addition to them without adequate remuneration or extensions of credit facilities or banking services.
2. Members shall neither prepare nor place any advertisement in any medium, which

    (a) is knowingly a copy or a plagiarism of any other advertisement of any kind whatsoever;
    (b) makes attacks of a personal character, or makes uncalled for reflections on competitors or competitive goods;
    (c) is indecent, vulgar, suggestive, repulsive or offensive either in theme or treatment;
    (d) is objectionable medical advertising and an offer of free medical treatment; advertising that makes remedial relief or curative claims, either directly or by inference, not justified by the facts of common experience;
    (e) concerns a product, known to the member to contain habit-forming or dangerous drugs.

Or any advertisement which may cause money loss to the reader, or injury in health or morals or loss of confidence in reputable advertising and honourable business or which is regarded by the Executive Committee of the Advertising Agencies Association of India, as unworthy.

In the event of a member proving to the satisfaction of the Executive Committee that a client has withdrawn his Account on the grounds of the Member's refusal to undertake unethical advertising (as described above) no other Member shall accept any business whatever from the said client.

ANNEXURE III

THE CODE FOR COMMERCIAL ADVERTISING ON DOORDARSHAN

Definitions

In this Code, unless the context otherwise requires—

(i) "Government" means, Government of India.

(ii) "Director General" means, the Director General, Doordarshan or any officer duly authorized by him on his behalf and includes the Director, Doordarshan Kendras.

(iii) "Advertiser" means any individual or organization including a commercial concern which has offered any advertisement for telecast over television.

(iv) "Advertising Agency" means any organization which is accredited to, recognized by or registered with Doordarshan as such.

(v) "Advertisement" includes any item of publicity for goods or services inserted in the programme telecast by Doordarshan with a view to increasing sales.

(vi) "Spot Advertisement" means any direct advertisement mentioning products/services, their merits and other related details.

(vii) "Advertising Association" means an Association or Society or any other body of whose constituent members are Advertising Agencies registered/recognized or accredited to Doordarshan.

Scope

(a) The Director General, Doordarshan, shall be the sole judge of the suitability or otherwise of an advertisement for telecast and his decision in this regard shall be final.

(b) Doordarshan time shall be sold to the Advertisers/Advertising Agencies at the sole discretion of the Director General, Doordarshan, according to the prescribed rates.

(c) The advertisement should be clearly distinguishable from the programme by using suitable wipes/blank, in order to avoid the message of the programme getting mixed up with the content and images of the advertisement.

I. Introduction

Advertising is an important legitimate means for the seller to awaken interest in his goods and services. The success of advertising depends on public confidence. Hence no practice should be permitted which tends to impair this confidence. The standards laid down here should be taken as minimum standards of acceptability which would be liable to be reviewed from time to time in relation to the prevailing norm of viewers' susceptibilities.

The following standards of conduct are laid down in order to develop and promote healthy advertising practices in Doordarshan. Responsibility for the observance of these rules rests equally upon the Advertiser and the Advertising Agency.

All those engaged in advertising are strongly recommended to familiarize themselves with the legislation affecting advertising in this country, particularly the following Acts and the Rules framed under them :

(1) Drugs and Cosmetics Act, 1940.
(2) Drugs Control Act, 1950.
(3) Drugs and Magic Remedies (Objectionable Advertisements) Act, 1954.
(4) Copyright Act, 1957.
(5) Trade and Merchandise Marks Act, 1958.
(6) Prevention of Food Adulteration Act, 1954.
(7) Pharmacy Act, 1948.
(8) Prize Competition Act, 1955.
(9) Emblems and Names (Prevention of Improper Use) Act, 1950.
(10) Consumer Protection Act, 1986.
(11) Indecent Representation of Women (Prohibition) Act, 1986.

(12) AIR/Doordarshan Code.
(13) Code of Ethics for Advertising in India issued by the Advertising Council of India (see Annexure I).
(14) Code of Standards in Relation to Advertising of Medicine and Treatments (see Annexure II).
(15) Standards of Practice for Advertising Agencies (see Annexure III).

(The list is illustrative and not exhaustive.)

II. The Code

General Rules of Conduct in Advertising :

1. Advertising shall be so designed as to conform to the laws of the country and should not offend against morality, decency and religious susceptibilities of the people.
2. No advertisement shall be permitted which—

   (i) derides any race, caste, colour, creed and nationality;
   (ii) is against any of the directive principles, or any other provision of the Constitution of India;
   (iii) tends to incite people to crime, cause disorder or violence, or breach of law or glorifies violence or obscenity in any way;
   (iv) presents criminality as desirable;
   (v) adversely affects friendly relations with foreign States;
   (vi) exploits the national emblem, or any part of the Constitution or the person or personality of a national leader or State Dignitary;
   (vii) relates to or promotes cigarettes and tobacco products, liquor, wines and other intoxicants;
   (viii) in its depiction of women violates the constitutional guarantees to all citizens such as equality of status and opportunity and dignity of the individual. In particular, no advertisement shall be permitted which projects a derogatory image of women. Women must not be portrayed in a manner that emphasizes passive, submissive qualities and encourages them to play a subordinate, secondary role in the family and society.

The portrayal of men and women should not encourage mutual disrespect between the sexes. Advertiser shall ensure that the portrayal of the female form is tasteful and aesthetic, and is within the well established norms of good taste and decency.

3. No advertisement message shall in any way be presented as News.
4. No advertisement shall be permitted the objects whereof are wholly or mainly of a religious or political nature; advertisements must not be directed towards any religious or political and/or have any relation to any industrial dispute.
5. Advertisements for services concerned with the following shall not be accepted :

   (i) Money lenders;
   (ii) Chit funds;
   (iii) Saving schemes and lotteries other than those conducted by Central and State Government Organizations, Nationalized or recognized banks and Public Sector Undertakings;
   (iv) Matrimonial agencies;
   (v) Unlicensed employment services;
   (vi) Fortune tellers or soothsayers etc., and those with claims of hypnotism;
   (vii) Foreign goods and foreign banks;
   (viii) Betting tips and guide books etc., relating to horse-racing, or other games of chance.

6. The items advertised shall not suffer from any defect or deficiency as mentioned in Consumer Protection Act, 1986.
7. No advertisement shall contain references which are likely to lead the public to infer that the product advertised or any of its ingredients has some special or miraculous or super-natural property or quality, which is difficult of being proved, e.g. cure for baldness, skin whitener, etc.
8. No advertisement shall contain the words 'Guarantee' or 'Guaranteed', etc. unless the full terms of the guarantee

are available for inspection by the Director General, Doordarshan, and are clearly set out in the advertisement and are made available to the purchaser in writing at the point of sale or with the goods. In all cases terms must include details of the remedial action available to the purchaser. No advertiser shall contain a direct or implied reference to any guarantee which purports to take away or diminish the legal rights of a purchaser.

9. Scientific or statistical excerpts from technical literature etc., may be used only with a proper sense of responsibility to the ordinary viewer. Irrelevant data and scientific jargon shall not be used to make claims appear to have a scientific basis they do not possess. Statistics of limited validity should not be presented in a way as to make it appear that they are universally true.
10. Advertisers or their agents must be prepared to produce evidence to substantiate any claims or illustrations. The Director General reserves the right to ask for such proofs and get them examined to his full satisfaction. In case of goods covered by mandatory quality control orders, the advertiser shall produce a quality certificate from the institutions recognized by the Government for this purpose.
11. Advertisements shall not contain disparaging or derogatory references to another product or service.
12. Imitation likely to mislead viewers shall be avoided.
13. Visual and verbal representation of actual and comparative prices and costs shall be accurate and shall not mislead on account of undue emphasis or distortion.
14. Testimonials must be genuine and used in a manner not to mislead the viewers. Advertisers or Advertising Agencies must be prepared to produce evidence in support of their claims.
15. The picture and the audible matter of the advertisement shall not be excessively 'loud'. This is to ensure that between the programme and the advertisement there is a smooth changeover avoiding jerkiness or shock to the viewers.
16. No advertisement of any kind of jewellery or precious stones shall be accepted.

17. Information to consumers in matters of weight, quality or prices of products where given shall be accurate.
18. Advertisements indicating price comparisons or reductions must comply with relevant laws.
19. No advertisement shall be accepted which violates AIR and TV Broadcast Code which is reproduced below :

GENERAL AIR/TV CODE

(1) Criticism of friendly countries;
(2) attack on religions or communities;
(3) anything obscene or defamatory;
(4) incitement to violence or anything against maintenance of law and order;
(5) anything amounting to contempt of court;
(6) aspersions against the integrity of the President and Judiciary;
(7) anything affecting the integrity of the Nation; and
(8) criticism by name of any person.

20. Any such effects which might startle the viewing public must not be incorporated in advertisements. For example, and without limiting the scope, the use of the following sound effects will not be permitted :

Rapid gunfire or rifle shots
Sirens
Bombardments
Screams
Raucous laughter and the like.

21. Any pretence in advertising copy must be avoided and such copy shall not be accepted by Doordarshan Kendras. The 'simulation' of appearance or video of a personality in connection with advertisements for commercial products is also prohibited unless bonafide evidence is available that such personality has given permission for the simulation and it is clearly understood that stations telecasting such announcements are indemnified by the advertiser or advertising agency against any possible legal action.

Advertising and Children

22. No advertisement for a product or service shall be accepted if it suggests in any way that unless the children themselves buy or encourage other people to buy the products or services, they will be failing in their duty or lacking in loyalty to any person or organization.
23. No advertisement shall be accepted which leads children to believe that if they do not own or use the product advertised they will be inferior in some way to other children or that thay are liable to be condemned or ridiculed for not owning or using it.
24. Any advertisement which endangers the safety of the children or creates in them any interest in unhealthy practices, shall not be accepted, e.g. playing in the middle of the road, leaning dangerously out of a window,. playing with match boxes and other goods which can cause accidents.
25. Children shall not be shown begging or in an undignified or indecent manner.
26. No advertisement likely to bring advertising into contempt or disrepute shall be permitted. Advertising shall not take advantage of the superstition or ignorance of the general public.
27. No advertisements of talismans, charms and character reading from photographs or such matters as well as those which trade on the superstition of general public shall be permitted.
28. Advertising shall be truthful, avoid distorting facts and misleading the public by means of implications and omissions. For instance, it shall not mislead the consumer by false statements, as to :

    (i) the character of the merchandise i.e. its utility, materials, ingredients, origin, etc.
    (ii) the price of the merchandise, its value, its suitability or terms of purchase.
    (iii) the services accompanying purchase, including delivery, exchange, return, repair, upkeep, etc.
    (iv) personal recommendations of the article or service.

The quality or the value of competing goods or the trustworthiness of statements made by others.

29. Testimonials of any kind from experts, etc. other than Government recognized standardization agencies shall not be permitted.
30. No advertisement shall be permitted to contain any claim so exaggerated as to lead inevitably to disappointment in the minds of the public.
31. Methods of advertising designed to create confusion in the mind of the consumer as between goods by one maker and another maker are unfair and shall not be used. Such methods may consist in :

    (i) the imitation of the trademark or name of competition or the packaging or labelling of goods; or
    (ii) the imitation of advertising devices, copy, layout or slogans.

32. Indecent, vulgar, suggestive, repulsive or offensive themes or treatment shall be avoided in all advertisements. This also applies to such advertisements which in themselves are not objectionable as defined above, but which advertise objectionable books, photographs or other matter and thereby lead to their sale and circulation.
33. No advertisement in respect of medicines and treatments shall be accepted which is in contravention of the Code relating to Standards for advertising of medicines and treatments as per Annexure II.

Note I. In all other respects, the Director General will be guided for purposes of commercial telecasting in Doordarshan by the Code of Ethics for Advertising in India as modified from time to time (relevant excerpts appended at Annexure I).

Note II. Notwithstanding anything contained herein, this Code is subject to such modifications/directions as may be made/ issued by the Director General from time to time.

Note III. All advertising agencies shall adhere to the standards of practice as prescribed by Advertising Agencies

Association of India, Bombay, as given in Annexure III.

III. Procedure for the Enforcement of the Code

1. Complaints or reports on contraventions of the Code, received by Doordarshan may in the first instance be referred by Director General to the Advertisers' Association(s) concerned with request for suitable action.
2. If complaints under the Code cannot be satisfactorily resolved at association(s)'s level, they shall be reported to the Director General who will then consider suitable action.
3. For any complaints under the Code received by Doordarshan concerning a party outside the purview of the various member association(s), the Director General will draw attention of such party to the complaint and where necessary, take suitable action on his own.

Annexure I

Excerpts from the Code of Ethics for Advertising in India Issued by the Advertising Council of India

Introduction

Along with the development of a very complex distribution system, the requirements of a market economy, faced with the need for ensuring a regular flow of mass production, have given rise to the development of new techniques of sales promotion.

Of these, advertising has proved itself to be of inestimable value for producers and distributors as well as for consumers. It enables the former to maintain contact with customers who are widely scattered and often unknown, and it assists the latter in choosing those goods and services that are the best suited to their particular requirements.

Advertising has become an important social and economic force in the world today. It is, therefore, essential that any unfair advertising practice likely to alienate public confidence would be eliminated. Hence the need for rules of conduct drawn up for the purpose of preventing possible abuses and of promoting and increasing sense of responsibility towards the consumer on the part of the advertisers, advertising agencies and media owners and suppliers.

Recognizing that the legitimate function of advertising is the advocacy of the merits of particular products or services, this code is intended to be applied in the spirit as well as in the letter and should be taken to set out the minimum standards to be observed by the parties concerned. This Code does override all ethical standards in advertising laid down by individual organizations, but it does not supersede the standards of practice laid down by individual organizations as incumbent upon their own members and applying to their own particular trade or industry.

Annexure II

Code of Standards in Relation to the Advertising of Medicines and Treatments

This Code has been drafted for the guidance of advertisers, manufacturers, distributors, advertising agents, publishers and suppliers or various advertising media. The harm to the individual that may result from exaggerated, misleading or unguaranteed claims justified the adoption of a very high standard and the inclusion of considerable detail in a Code to guide those who are concerned with this form of advertising. Newspaper and other advertising media are urged not to accept advertisements in respect of any product or treatment from any advertiser or advertising agent who disregards the provisions of this Code in any form of advertising or publicity relating to the product or treatment. The provisions of this Code do not apply to an advertisement published by or under the authority of a Government, Ministry or Department, nor to an advertisement published in journals circulated to Registered Medical Practitioners, Registered Dentists, Registered Pharmacists or Registered Nurses.

Section I

General Principles

1. *Cure* : No advertisement should contain a claim to cure any ailment or symptoms of ill-health, nor should any advertisement contain a word or expression used in such

a form or context as to mean in the positive sense the extirpation of any ailment, illness or disease.

2. *Illness, etc. properly requiring medical attention* : No advertisement should contain any matter which can be regarded as offer of medicine or product for, or advice relating to, the treatment of serious diseases, complaints, conditions, indications or symptoms which should rightly receive the attention of a Registered Medical Practitioner (see Sec. 2).
3. *Misleading or exaggerated claims* : No advertisement should contain any matter which directly or by implication misleads or departs from the truth as to the composition, character or action of the medicine or treatment advertised or as to its suitability for the purpose for which it is recommended.
4. *Appeals to fear* : No advertisement should be calculated to induce fear on the part of the reader that he is suffering, or may without treatment suffer from an ailment, illness or diseases.
5. *Diagnosis or treatment by correspondence* : No advertise-ment should offer to diagnose by correspondence disease, conditions or any symptoms of ill-health in a human being or request from any person or a statement of his or any other person's symptoms of ill-health with a view to advertising as to or providing for treatment of such conditions of ill-health by correspondence. Nor should any advertisement offer to treat by correspondence any ailment, illness, disease or symptoms thereof in a human being.
6. *Disparaging references*: No advertisement should directly or by implication disparage the products, medicines or treatments of another advertiser or manufacturer or registered medical practitioner or the medical profession.
7. *College, clinic, institute, laboratory* : No advertisement should contain these or similar terms unless an establishment corresponding with the description used does in fact exist.
8. *Doctors, hospitals, etc.* : No advertisement should contain any reference to doctors or hospitals, whether Indian or foreign, unless such reference can be

substantiated by independent evidence and can properly be used in the manner proposed.

9. *Products offered particularly to women* : No advertisement of products, medicines or treatments of disorders or irregularities peculiar to women should contain expression which may imply that the product, medicine or treatment advertised can be effective in inducing miscarriage.
10. *Family planning* : Advertisements for measures or apparatus concerning family planning would be permissible in so far as they conform to the generally accepted national policy in this behalf.
11. *Illustrations* : No advertisement should contain any illustration which by itself or in combination with words used in connection therewith is likely to convey a misleading impression, or of the reasonable inference to be drawn from such advertisement infringes any of the provisions of this Code.
12. *Exaggerated copy* : No advertisement should contain copy which is exaggerated by reason of improper use of words, phrases or methods of presentation, e.g., the use of the words "magic, magical, miracle, miraculous".
13. *Natural remedies* : No advertisement should claim or suggest contrary to the fact, that the article advertised is in the form in which it occurs in nature or that its value lies in its being a "natural" product.
14. *Special claims* : No advertisement should contain any reference which is calculated to lead the public to assume that the article, product, medicine or treatment advertised has some special property or quality which is in fact unknown or unrecognized.
15. *Sexual weakness, premature ageing, loss of virility* : No advertisement should claim that the product, medicine, or treatment advertised will promote sexual virility or be effective in treating sexual weakness or habits associated with sexual excess or indulgence or any ailment, illness or disease associated with those habits. In particular, such terms as "premature ageing", "loss of virility", will be regarded as conditions for which medicines, products, appliances or treatment may not be advertised.

16. *Slimming, weight reduction or limitation or figure control* : No advertisement should offer any medical product for the purpose of slimming, weight reduction or limitation or figure control. Medical products intended to reduce appetite will usually be regarded as being for slimming purposes.
17. *Tonics* : The use of this expression in advertisements should not imply that the product or medicine can be used in the treatment of sexual weakness.
18. *Hypnosis* : No advertisement should contain any offer to diagnose or treat complaints or conditions by hypnosis.
19. *Materials to students* : Materials meant for distribution in educational institutions must not carry advertisement of anything other than those of value to students.

Section II

Restrictions Imposed by Statute on Advertising of Medicines and Treatments

1. Rule 106 of the Drug Rules, 1945, provides that : no drug may convey to the intending user thereof any idea that it may prevent or cure, one or more of the diseases or ailments specified in Schedule J.

SCHEDULE J

Blindness	Bright's Disease	Cancer
Cataract	Deafness	Delayed Menstruation
Diabetes	Epilepsy	Hydrocele
Infantile Paralysis	Leprosy	Leucoderma
Lockjaw	Locomotor Ataxia	Insanity
Tuberculosis	Tumors	Venereal Diseases (in general)
Female Diseases (in general)	Fevers (in general)	Fits
Glaucoma	Goitre	Gonorrhea
	Soft Cancer	
Heart Diseases	High Blood Pressure	Lupus
Obesity	Paralysis	Plague
Rupture	Sexual Impotence	Small Pox

2. No drug may purport to claim to procure or assist to procure, or may convey to the intending user thereof any idea that it may procure or assist to procure miscarriage in women.

Definition

'Drug' includes for internal or external use for human beings or animals all substances intended to be used for or in the treatment, mitigation, or prevention of disease in human beings or animals, other than medicines and substances exclusively used or prepared for use in accordance with the Ayurvedic or Unani system of medicines.

Annexure III

Standards of Practice for Advertising Agencies

(As approved by the Advertising Agencies Association of India, Bombay.)

1. Every member of the Association shall carry on his profession and business in such a manner as to uphold the dignity and interests of the Association.
2. Every member shall refrain from canvassing Advertisers or prospective Advertisers in such a way as to reflect detrimentally upon Advertising Agents as a whole or this Association or any Advertising Agent in particular.
3. Canvassing is permitted subject to the condition that a member may make known to the client of another member its own capabilities as an Advertising Agency but may not submit a specific report or detailed recommendations concerning the client's advertising unless so requested by him in writing.
4. No member shall pay or undertake to pay or allow to an advertiser or his agent or representative, the whole or any portion of the standard rate of commission resulting or to result to such member from an advertising medium nor promise or procure or undertake to procure advertising space or facilities free of charge, to any advertising, or at a reduced rate, nor supply free or partly

free to any advertiser, any advertising material, including finished drawings, or other art work, photographs, blocks, stereos, matrices or the like, type-setting or printing nor defray in whole or in part the salary of any employee of an advertiser, nor grant any allowances, discount or the like nor render any service having the effect of rebating the commission allowed by an advertising medium. The sharing of commission with member or overseas agency, or with agent by this Association shall, however, be permitted.

5. The practice of submitting speculative campaigns is unhealthy to the growth of the advertising services and no speculative campaign shall be submitted by any member of the Advertising Agencies Association of India. By speculative campaign, it is meant, producing a campaign unsolicited by an advertiser and equally producing a campaign where the advertiser had requested one or more advertising agencies to do so, unaccompanied by a firm offer of business. That members shall notify the Secretary of the Association if any such queries were made by prospective advertiser, and that such information shall be circulated by the Secretary to all members.
6. Any member relinquishing an Account on the ground of slow payment, doubtful credit or incurring a bad debt, shall immediately notify the Secretary of the Association and such information shall be circulated in strictest confidence for information and protection of other members.
7. No business shall be accepted which is conditional upon the payment of commission or fee or reward to a third party not a full-time employee of the members either for introducing the business or for services in connection with the account thereafter. This rule, however, shall not preclude a member from employing copy-writers or production men at fees commensurate with the values of their work.

Obligations to Clients

1. Member Agencies must continue to render full agency

service in reasonable conformity to the Association's Agency Service Standards.

2. Members shall retain either commission granted by media owners or charge the clients a service fee which shall never be less than 15 per cent of the client's gross expenditure.
3. Nor shall they supply material for advertising on any basis that can be considered as direct or indirect or secret rebating. Where no commission is allowed by the media owner, the member will charge his clients a minimum of 15 per cent on the gross cost.
4. Members will not accept discounts or commission, other than the regular agency commission allowed by the publishers without the client's knowledge and consent.
5. Members shall at all times use their best efforts to obtain for their clients the lowest rate to which such clients are entitled.

Obligations to Suppliers

Members shall take all steps to assure themselves as to the financial soundness of their clients.

Obligations to Fellow Agencies

1. Members are required to use fair methods of competition; not to offer the services enumerated above or services in addition to them without adequate remuneration or extension of credit facilities or banking services.
2. Members shall neither prepare nor place any advertisement in any medium, which

   (a) is knowingly a copy or a plagiarism of any other advertisement of any kind whatsoever;
   (b) makes attacks of a personal character, or makes uncalled for reflections on competitors or competitive goods;
   (c) is indecent, vulgar, suggestive, repulsive or offensive either in theme or treatment;
   (d) is objectionable medical advertising and an offer of

free medical treatment, advertising that makes remedial or curative claims, either directly or by inference, not justified by the facts of common experience;

(e) concerns a product, known to the member to contain habit-forming or danger drugs; or any advertisement which may cause money loss to the reader, or injury in health or morals or loss of confidence in reputable advertising and honourable business or which is regarded by the Executive Committee of the Advertising Agencies Association of India, as unworthy. In the event of a member proving to the satisfaction of the Executive Committee that a client has withdrawn his Account on the grounds of the member's refusal to undertake unethical advertising (as described above) no other member shall accept any business whatever from the said client.

ANNEXURE IV

EXCERPTS FROM INTER-DEPARTMENTAL COMMITTEE ON INTRODUCING COMPETITION IN THE ELECTRONIC MEDIA

The Committee recognises the importance of introducing competition in the Electronic Media to provide additional outlets to the creative talent, to strengthen the democratic fabric of the nation and help better in meeting the cultural aspirations of different regions.

There is need to guard against the dangers of unrestrained commercialism which may follow the establishment of additional channels financed solely through advertising. The dangers of control of these media falling into the hands of unscrupulous or anti-national elements also should not be discounted.

In regard to approach to the new broadcasting system the following recommendations have been made :

(i) Subject to viability of operations, preference should be given to setting up new TV/Radio channels in different parts of the country for regional broadcasts. These transmitters can, over a period of time, link-up suitably either by forming a consortium or by entering into suitable arrangements amongst themselves. Such a link-up would provide inter-regional network.

(ii) (a) Simultaneously, the second Doordarshan channels in the four metropolitan cities can be leased out to suitable licencees.

(b) Also simultaneously, additional radio channels including FM stations wherever available may also be similarly leased out.

These actions under this option should be taken only after suitable legislation is passed.

Relevant excerpts from the recommendations made by the Inter-departmental Committee on Introducing Competition in the Electronic Media, October 1991 (Vardan Committee).

(iii) The option to permit one agency or consortium to set up a series of transmitters in the country will, in the opinion of the Committee, rank only next to the option of permitting a number of licencees to set up different TV/Radio transmitters in the country.

(iv) The Committee does not recommend leasing out a particular chunk of time from an existing TV/Radio channel.

(v) The option of a licencee leasing a transponder on a satellite for satellite-derived direct broadcast would perhaps be appropriate for developmental or educational telecast. The Committee notes that as of now there is no such spare space segment available. As and when one becomes available, the Government can take an appropriate decision.

The Committee feels that in view of the sensitive nature of the choice, the selection of agencies for grant of licence should be performed by an independent agency in transparent manner. It feels that the organisations eligible to receive licences should be public limited companies with major interest groups concerned with broadcasting represented in management and with open access to shareholding. Such organisations should be willing to abide by guidelines to be prescribed by the government regarding their functioning. Certain cross media restrictions are recommended in order to avoid monopoly over information sources. Preference may be given to public bodies like universities, cooperative institutions, etc. if they apply for licences.

The Committee has suggested that the Broadcasting Council of India to be constituted through a legislation, amending the relevant sections in the Prasar Bharati Act, be entrusted with the functions of licensing, monitoring of programmes and quality rating.

The Committee has recommended that a new legislation be enacted to govern the setting up and operation of additional broadcast channels, and has outlined the areas where such legislation will be required.

ANNEXURE V

EXCERPTS FROM NATIONAL MEDIA POLICY : A WORKING PAPER*

Objectives

The National Media Policy should lay the broad framework of the relationship of the Government with both national and international media such as Television (domestic, foreign and cable), Video, Internet, Radio, Newspaper, Film, etc. Its broad objective should be to help a citizen of the country to realise his or her potential best. The reach of print media is limited to the literate people only, whereas the Electronic Media—Radio and Television—has entered the house-holds of the people all over the country. Thus, it has the viewership of all kind—adult as well as minor, illiterate as well as literate, poor as well as rich. Slightly different is the approach of film media which has also the viewership of both illiterate and literate, but its viewership is basically voluntary. Its visual impact though is much more than that of print media on both educated as well as uneducated.

Accordingly, the Sub-Committee proposes the following objectives :

Not to permit growth of monopoly in any media;
To project the developmental needs and social, cultural and economic aspirations of the people, particularly in the rural areas who constitute a bulk of our population;
To strengthen, preserve and promote our democratic traditions, culture and values, national integration and scientific temper;
To promote and strengthen sense of national integrity

---

*Submitted by the Sub-Committee of the Consultative Committee of the Ministry of Information & Broadcasting on 29 March 1996.

built on secularism, socio-cultural pluralism and linguistic diversities (unity in diversity);

To facilitate greater access to information, education and entertainment in that order to all sections of the people;

To enable development in the wake of challenges thrown up by rapid technology;

To provide wider choice to the people in matters of information and entertainment;

To act as catalysts for social change;

To broadly ensure that discrimination based on gender, religion, caste, language, etc. is not directly or indirectly practiced or promoted and portrayal of any section of the society is not done in a derogatory manner.

Nature of Media Policy

As regards the question as to whether there should be a single media policy covering all media or separate for each of them, we need to look at the present status of various media. As far as the print media is concerned, it is in the private hands and Government has no direct role in its functioning. It is also pertinent to note that the reach of print media is only to the literate people and that too in urban areas in particular. There is Press Council of India to oversee the activities of the print media so that its functions within the given parameters laid down in the various enactments and the Constitution of India. Also, the Sub-Committee notes that the Press, over a period of time, jealously guards its freedom and is the most popular vehicle for dissent and pluralism in views.

Regarding film media, it is also largely in private hands and Government's control is only about certifying the cinematographic films which are screened for the public exhibition. The development of theatres to facilitate the proper exhibition of films to all categories of the people is also one of the aspects looked into by the Government. The reach of the film media is to both literate as well as illiterate, the same as electronic media, but the decision to see a film is a voluntary act as it requires money and time on the part of the viewers.

As stated above, electronic media has a global reach. It reaches not only within the boundaries of the country but by modern technology and innovation of satellite, it can reach to any remotest area of the world subject to the uplinking facilities. At present, the electronic media is controlled by the Government but that is applicable only in case of country based programmes, whereas there is no control on the programmes which are beamed through satellite by foreign lands in the country.

In the light of the above, it may appear that various media are so divergent that a single media policy may be difficult. The Sub-Committee had considered this question in detail and felt that the objectives chosen are general in nature and can be applicable for all the media. Therefore, it recommends that at macro-level, there should be a single media policy encompassing all the three media—print, film and electronic, but at operational level, each media should have its own detailed guidelines according to its reach, viewership/listeners/readership as the case may be.

Summary of Recommendations

Electronic Media

The broadcasting should observe *a greater degree of responsibility and sensitivity to Indian culture and ethos and cater to the developmental requirement of the country.* It should achieve an Indian personality in telecasting/broadcasting.

There *should be a regulatory body to* oversee both public and private telecasting/broadcasting. In this connection, the Sub-Committee noted that the provisions of the Prasar Bharati Act, which was unanimously passed by Parliament in 1990 should be kept in mind while framing the regulatory mechanism which should *be an independent autonomous authority.* The Sub-Committee is of confirmed opinion that no recourse should be taken by the Government to dilute the provision of the Prasar Bharati Act, 1990. This regulatory body may be set up to ensure adherence to the programmes/advertisement codes and other stipulations. This body or similar independent body may also develop an effective mechanism for public grievance redressal as well as implementation of its recommendations in respect of such grievances.

Adequate care should be taken to enable the setting up of non-commercial broadcasting stations to be run by universities, educational institutions, panchayats/local bodies, State Governments, etc.

The Sub-Committee recognises that for public broadcasting, adequate funding in the form of state support is necessary. The content of programmes or software is often dictated by the funding and therefore the Sub-Committee strongly recommends that this aspect should receive the attention of the government and an institutional system be worked out.

The national broadcasters—Akashvani and Doordarshan—should bear the responsibility to offer a high quality public service broadcasting that informs, educates and entertains the people and also provide coverage to national events like the Republic Day Parade. Taking into account the reach of the national broadcasters, primacy and exclusive responsibility should be provided to them in the matter of coverage of national events like Republic Day Parade, Independence Day, the President's Address to both the Houses of Parliament, etc.

The rights/obligations and exclusivity of the national broadcasters should be codified through law.

Whereas the broad policy approach should be the same for radio and television, minor variations/differences can be made in view of the difference in reach and impact of the two media. Programme/advertisement codes should be similar, if not, same. The viewer/listener interest should be kept in mind while spacing the advertisements. A new production style, which is people-oriented should be developed.

In tune with the policy framework suggested here, the Indian private sector/State Government/NGOs/Local Self Government should be allowed to enter the field of broadcasting/telecasting.

Appropriate provisions must be made to ensure that the control of private broadcasting does not fall in the hands of companies having major stake in the print medium or vice-versa. Cross-media ownership restrictions must, therefore, be considered.

Direct or indirect foreign equity participation in companies entering the field of private broadcasting should not be permitted.

Access on the private channel should be available to the common man through appropriate provisions in the law.

In view of the Supreme Court's Judgement on airwaves, an

independent authority must be set up to control and regulate the use of airwaves. The Sub-Committee felt that the integrity of the Indian Skies is as important as her territorial integrity. This regulatory authority must be set up through a law enacted by the Parliament at the earliest. This Body can combine the functions of the regulatory body mentioned in para 6.4.1.2 or can be a separate body exclusively for controlling the sky waves under the regulatory body mentioned in para 6.4.1.2.

The apex regulatory body should be an independent autonomous public authority representative of all sections and interests in the society and should control and regulate the use of air waves in the interests of the public and to prevent invasion of their rights.

The foreign satellite channels must also be brought within the ambit of the said regulatory body in order to make them amenable to the Indian laws.

The Sub-Committee felt that in the case of skywaves, efforts should be made to develop an international convention to forge multilateral/agreements with countries especially in regard to software.

The Sub-Committee noted that it will be difficult to pre-censor programmes aired on television in view of vast structure such a step would call for. By bringing in the private broadcasting/foreign channels within the purview of the Indian legal system, much of *laissez-faire* that exists can be curbed.

The Sub-Committee felt that the present programming in electronic media, especially television, needs to be more decentralised to meet the regional/local aspirations. In this connection, the Verghese Committee recommendations regarding decentralised programming, programme autonomy and constitution of five zones for this purpose (viz. South, West, Central, Eastern and North) should be considered by the Government.

Care should be taken that no monopoly is developed by the private broadcasters, by restructuring the number of channels, especially 'several interest' channels owned by them.

ANNEXURE VI

EXCERPTS FROM THE SENGUPTA COMMITTEE REPORT

Unparalleled changes have taken place in broadcasting throughout the world. The boundaries between broadcasting, telecommunications and information technologies are becoming blurred. We have also witnessed *rapid and fundamental changes in India's media scenario in recent years, driven by technological developments, economic reforms and liberalisation and the demands of increas-ingly discerning audiences*. We have already entered the era of choice and competition. The conventional and rigid regulations of yesteryears in the realm of broadcasting have become ineffective and impractical. The new technologies have demolished the monopoly of State-run electronic media and rendered redundant the regulations. Loosening of controls is a global phenomenon. On the other hand, the satellite revolution launched by the global giants, not to speak of some enterprising Indian entrepreneurs, is not an unmixed blessing. The unfettered freedom enjoyed by the foreign satellite channels and their lack of sensitivity to Indian culture and ethos as also the ersatz culture promoted by other private channels are matters of continuing concern to people.

Both Akashvani and Doordarshan have attempted with mixed success to adjust themselves with the fast changing scenario. They have had a remarkable record in public service broadcasting. They are the major cultural patrons of music, drama and the visual arts. They have no peers as surveyors of messages intended to support and stimulate socio-economic development. But what tended to undermine the image of these so called official media was the impression that had gained ground over the years that they could be influenced by those who wished to manipulate them for their own needs, whether it is the government of the day or other

---

Excerpts from the Sengupta Committee Report on Prasar Bharati, submitted in August 1996.

interested groups. The vociferous demand for granting autonomy to the electronic media and thus insulating them against external pressures ultimately led to the promulgation of the Prasar Bharati Act of 1990. The postulates that guided the Act have been overtaken by several events of the nineties especially the emergence of transnational broadcasting and the two separate but concurring landmark judgements on airwaves by the Supreme Court in February, 1995 holding *inter alia* that airwaves of frequencies were a public property and that broadcasting media should be under the control of the public as distinct from the Government.

We noticed an overwhelming consensus in favour of freeing airwaves from Government monopoly, thereby allowing Indian broadcasters the facility of uplinking from Indian soil. Such a consensus is absent in regard to foreign satellite channels, although there is a body of opinion in favour of this. We also noted that mere denial of permission to a foreign channel does not prevent it from broadcasting programmes directly to Indian homes with the help of uplinking facilities from other countries.

As a sequel to the landmark judgement of the Supreme Court declaring the airwaves as a public property, there is urgent need for establishing a suitable regulatory framework for the multiplicity of channels likely to emerge on the audio-visual landscape in the near future. An authority to grant frequencies and franchises and regulate the licensees, has to be created to ensure that there is no unfair or unjust treatment and unwarranted infringement of privacy or violation of accepted standards of public taste and decency. We strongly endorse the recommendation of the Paswan Sub-Committee for setting up an independent apex body to regulate and monitor airwaves. We propose *setting up a Radio and Television Authority of India*, an independent body which is not part of Prasar Bharati. On the contrary, Prasar Bharati being one of the many players in the Indian broadcasting arena, will also be overseen by the Authority as far as the 'complaints function' is concerned. The Authority will perform the following functions :

(i) Licensing of

(a) satellite uplinking
(b) terrestrial analog transmission of radio and television

(c) terrestrial digital transmission of radio and television
(d) multilex providers.

(ii) Prescribing programming obligations and programming standards to ensure quality and diversity.
(iii) Making arrangement for ascertaining and monitoring public opinion about the programmes and services and ascertaining the needs, interests and tastes of members of the public.
(iv) Determine the maximum limit for the quantum of advertising content so that advertisements are not obstrusive or jarring.
(v) Receive complaints of violation of norms of decency and of the Programming and Advertising Codes and adjudicate on them after hearing the parties concerned.

There is a school of thought which believes that terrestrial broadcasting should remain the monopoly of Doordarshan, as the National Broadcaster. We do not agree with this view. We have noticed that local TV stations have been competing very successfully with satellite channels in other countries. Why then should not such local terrestrial TV and radio stations be permitted in a country of India's vast size and diversity? The immediate fallout of allowing uplinking in respect of private broadcasters, both Indian and foreign and in permitting local terrestrial stations will be to create enormous job opportunities and also to bring handsome revenue to the nation.

We understand that Indian Broadcasters like JAIN, Sun TV and Asianet and others like Zee TV, Sony, ATN and BITV have been spending crores of rupees worth of foreign exchange in obtaining uplinking from places like Dubna in Russia, Subic Bay in the Philippines, Singapore and even Sri Lanka. This involves diversion of foreign exchange both by the satellite operators and by Indian companies who have to pay for advertising their products in their channels in foreign exchange. If and when they are allowed to uplink from Indian soil their expense will come down considerably and they will also avoid possible FERA violations. On the other hand, India may gain billions of dollars in foreign exchange through the licence fee and royalty payable by the foreign satellite channels and the advertising revenue that will come from companies outside India. Also this will bring about some real competition for Doordarshan. In the long run this will improve the competitive strength of Doordarshan and will also open up opportunities for news and current affairs programmes on foreign networks. Advertising tariff will substantially escalate as it will be guided by considerations like event marketing and popularity.

Another advantage of extending uplinking facilities to domestic and foeign satellite channels will be that they can be brought under the purview of Indian laws. While granting licences the Radio and Television Authority of India that has been envisaged will compel them to adhere to the prevalent Programming and Advertising Codes. The Authority will have the power to prevent telecasting of obscene 'adult' movies and enforce on the satellite channels the same guidelines that DD follows. Similarly, liquor advertisements can also be done away with. Fears have been expressed by some sections about the airing of antinational programmes or messages on private networks and possible violation of the standards of national security. But we feel such fears are not justified. It is much better to permit and control airwaves than letting them move around as free floating channels. The 1885 Telegraph Act aimed at checking misuse of airwaves has become outdated and requires to be recast. Before providing uplinking from Indian soil to a foreign party, the credentials of the party will have to be scrutinised.

We share the concern of the women's groups and activists about stereotyping of women and inequality in women's access to and participation in all communication systems specially in media which has been identified, and rightly so, as one of the critical areas for the advancement and empowerment of women. This is an area to which the proposed Radio and Televison Authority as well as Prasar Bharati should give due weightage.

This Group believes that Prasar Bharati, as the inheritor of the great tradition, should be the quintessential public service broadcaster. This is not to suggest that private broadcasters have no role to play in this sphere. Indeed, the private operators should have an obligation to put out programmes devoted to socially relevant themes and earmark certain slots for the purpose.

This Group recognises that for public broadcasting financial support from the Government is inevitable. We do not subscribe to the view that this might lead to an abridgement of the autonomy of Prasar Bharati, in any way, we are suggesting the revival of the Broadcast Receiver Licence (BRL) fee for TV sets. Such public funding will place on Prasar Bharati an obligation to be accountable to its clientele.

So far there has been very inadequate attention given to marketing in Akashvani and Doordarshan systems. First, our electronic media have to compete with invaders of the scene from the outside and the domestic competitors. Secondly, they will have to compete a great deal with each other. We have no doubt that this process will bring about a new motivation and all round innovativeness in both these organisations in creating as well as marketing new products and services. We notice that in recent months Akashvani has registered a significant improvement in its marketing activities resulting in earning of extra revenue, whereas Doordarshan has lagged behind in its marketing efforts in the last one or two years. Not only has it given up direct marketing, it appears to have gone for the softer option of franchising to others which accounts for the significant fall in its ad revenue compared to earlier years. We recommend that both the organisations should give a lot of importance to marketing. There should be one Deputy Managing Director each in Akashvani and Doordarshan for marketing. We also note that the Ministry has constituted a Committee to evolve suitable strategies for marketing airtime in Akashvani and Doordarshan. The strategies and recommendations made by this Committee will be of considerable use for Prasar Bharati in revamping their marketing.

Major recommendations of this Group are :

1. Prasar Bharati should be a Statutory Corporation as envisaged in the Act and can stand operating immediately. The preamble to the Act may be suitably amplified and the suggested modified version is reproduced hereunder : "An Act is to be provided for the establishment of a Broadcasting Corporation of India, to be known as Prasar Bharati for providing public service broadcasting and fulfil the basic information, education and entertainment needs of the people and to define its

composition, functions and powers and to provide for matters connected therewith or incidental thereto."

2. It is necessary to split Akashvani and Doordarshan into two completely separate wings under the corporate umbrella of the Prasar Bharati Corporation, with close coordination in areas clearly defined and delineated by the Corporation. For all practical purposes they should operate as separate entities. Steps should be taken to demarcate the hardware and the assets between Akashvani and Doordarshan and, bifurcate the personnel across all disciplines.
3. We recommend a full-time Chairman, instead of the part-time Chairman as envisaged in the Act, in the interest of autonomy and in view of the magnitude of the network of the two wings and expansion of their operations in the years to come. We also feel that the functions of the Chairman and of Chief Executive should be combined in one functionary i.e. the whole time Chairman.
4. We recommend six full-time and four part-time members of the Board, in addition to a representative from the Ministry of Information and Broadcasting not below the level of a Joint Secretary. The Managing Directors of Akashvani and Doordarshan will be Members of the Prasar Bharati Board representing radio and television, respectively.
5. We are of the firm opinion that the provision for two elected representatives of the employees of the Corporation on the Board is fraught with serious complications. The acrimony and disharmony likely to be generated by them.

ANNEXURE VII

GROSS COMMERCIAL REVENUE OF AKASHVANI AND DOORDARSHAN

Year	Akashvani			Doordarshan
	Vivid Bharati (Rs. Millions)	Primary Channel	Total	
1985-86	175.5	26.4	201.9	602.0
1986-87	177.2	62.8	240.0	933.1
1987-88	192.6	94.0	286.6	1363.0
1988-89	220.0	104.5	324.5	1612.6
1989-90	237.2	112.7	349.9	3101.3
1990-91	252.7	140.5	393.2	2538.5
1991-92	348.9	178.4	527.3	3006.1
1992-93	376.6	212.5	589.1	3602.3
1993-94	369.6	273.9	643.5	3729.5
1994-95	354.4	289.5	643.9	3980.0
1995-96	373.2	436.5	809.7	4301.3

ANNEXURE VIII

THE SATELLITE CHANNEL UNIVERSE

No.	Channel	Network	Owner	Satellite	Lang.	Programming	Launch date	%age
1	2	3	4	5	6	7	8	9
1	DD1			Insat-ID*	Hindi & English	Entertainment, current affairs	Aug. 1982	100
2	DD2			Insat-2B*	Hindi & English	Entertainment, current affairs	Apr. 1993	100
3	DD3			Terrestrial	Hindi & English	News, current affairs	Nov. 1995	100
4	DD4			Insat-2B*	Malayalam		Oct. 1993	100
5	DD5			Insat-2B*	Tamil		Aug. 1990	100
6	DD6			Insat-2D*	Oriya		Sept. 1991	100
7	DD7			Insat-2B*	Bengali		Nov. 1991	100
8	DD8			Insat-2B*	Telugu/Punjabi		Jan. 1987	100
9	DD9			Insat-2B*	Kannada		Nov. 1990	100
10	DD10	Doordarshan	The Government of India	Insat-2B*	Marathi	Entertainment	Aug. 1986	100
11	DD11			Insat-2B*	Gujarati		Dec. 1992	100
12	DD13			Insat-2B*	Assamese		Mar. 1991	100
13	DD14			Insat-2A*	Rajasthani		Oct. 1991	100
14	DD15			Insat-2A*	Hindi		Nov. 1993	100
15	DD16			Insat-2A*	Hindi		Oct. 1993	100
16	DD17			Insat-2A*	Hindi		Dec. 1994	100

Contd.

TABLE *(Contd.)*

1	2	3	4	5	6	7	8	9
17	DD-CNNI			Insat-2A	English	News, current affairs	Jan. 1993	100
18	DD INTL			Insat-2B	Hindi	Entertainment	Mar. 1995	100
19	DD MOVIE CLUB			PAS-4	Films	Apr. 1995		100
20	STAR PLUS			PAS-4	English	Entertainment	Aug. 1991	100
21	STAR MOVIES	News Corp.	Asiasat I	English	Films	Oct. 1994		100
22	STAR SPORTS		Asiasat I	English/Hindi	Sports	Aug. 1991		100
23	CHANNEL [V]	STAR TV		Asiasat I	English & Hindi	Music	May 1994	100
24	ZEE TV			Asiasat I	Hindi	Entertainment news	Dec. 1993	100
25	ZEE CINEMA		Asia Today	Asiasat I	Hindi	Films	Apr. 1995	100
26	EL TV			Asiasat I	Hindi	Entertainment	Dec. 1994	100
27	BBC WORLD	BBC	BBC	PAS-4	English	News	Aug. 1991	70
28	MTV	MTV	Viacom International	PAS-4	English & Hindi	Music	Feb. 1996	70
29	ESPN	ESPN	Walt Disney Co.	PAS-4	English	Sports	Oct. 1995	70
30	ABNI	ABN	ABN Indusind Media, & TV 18	PAS-4	English	Business news	Jan. 1996	70
31	ATN	ATN	Siddhartha Srivastava	Gorizont 41	Hindi	Film based entertainment	Nov. 1991	100
32	JAIN TV	JAIN TV	J.K. Jain	PAS-4	Hindi	Entertainment news religion	Jan. 1994	70
33	SONY	SONY	Sony Corp. & others	PAS-4	Hindi	Films, entertainment	Oct. 1995	70
34	CNN INTL	CNN	Time Warner-Turner Intl	PAS-4	English	News	Aug. 1995	70
35	INT CARTOON	CNN	Time Warner-Turner Intl	PAS-4	English	Films (8 hrs) cartoons (16 hrs)	Aug. 1995	70

Contd.

TABLE *(Contd.)*

1	2	3	4	5	6	7	8	9
36	DISCOVERY	Discovery	Cox Cable, TCI, UCT & NHBC	PAS-4	English & Hindi	Natural Sciences	Jun. 1995	70
37	SUN TV			Gorizont 41	Tamil	Entertainment	Mar. 1993	40
38	SUN MOVIES	Sun TV	Kalanidhi Maran	Gorizont 42	Tamil	Films	Jun. 1994	40
39	SUN MUSIC			Gorizont 42	Tamil	Music	Jan. 1994	40
40	UDAYA TV			Gorizont 42	Kannada	Films, entertainment	Oct. 1993	40
41	J JAY TV	J Jay TV	V. Baskaran	Gorizont 42	Tamil	Films, entertainment, politics	Apr. 1995	40
42	RAJ TV	Raj TV	M. Raajendran	Gorizont 41	Tamil	Fiims, ent., current affairs	Oct. 1994	40
43	VIJAY TV	Vijay TV	UB Group	Gorizont 41	Tamil	Entertainment	Nov. 1994	40
44	ASIANET	Asianet	Sashi Kumar & Raji Menon	Gorizont 42	Malayalam	Films, ent., current affairs	Aug. 1993	40
45	GEMINI TV	Gemini TV	Gemini Pictures Circuit	Gorizont 41	Telugu	Films, entertainment	Feb. 1994	40
46	ETV	ETV	Eenadu Publications	Intelsat 704	Telugu	Films, entertainment, news	Aug. 1995	Below20
47	NEPC	NEPC	NEPC Group	Intelsat 2	Hindi	Entertainment	Oct. 1995	Below20
48	YES	YES	Srishti Videocorp.	Intelsat 2	Hindi & English	Youth ent., education	Jun. 1995	Below20
49	TV PRIME	TVI	Business India Group	Stationar 3	Hindi & English	Entertainment, current affairs	Jul. 1995	Below20
50	MONEY TV	Money TV	Radhika Synth. & World Digital	Gorizont 42	English	Business news	Jan. 1996	Below20

Contd.

TABLE *(Contd.)*

1	2	3	4	5	6	7	8	9
51	VENUS TV	Venus TV	J. P. Shrivastava & Caroles	Ekran	Hindi	Agriculture, entertainment	To be launched	N.A.
52	HOME TV	Home TV	HTV, Pearson, Carlton & TVB	PAS-4	Hindi	Entertainment	May 1996	Below 20

* Available through terrestrial transmission

Source : Business Standard.

ANNEXURE IX

Bill No. 71 of 1997

THE BROADCASTING BILL, 1997

A

BILL

to provide for the establishment of an independent authority to be known as the Broadcasting Authority of India, for the purposes of facilitating and regulating broadcasting services in India and to provide for matters connected therewith or incidental thereto.

BE it enacted by Parliament in the Forty-eighth Year of the Republic of India as follows :

CHAPTER I

PRELIMINARY

Short title, extent and commencement

31. (*1*) This Act may be called the Broadcasting Act, 1997.

(*2*) It extends to the whole of India.

(*3*) It shall come into force on such date as the Central Government may, by notification in the Official Gazette, appoint.

Definitions

2. In this Act, unless the context otherwise requires :

25 of 1990

(a) "Aakashvani" shall have the same meaning as is assigned

to it in clause (a) of section 2 of the Prasar Bharati (Broadcasting Corporation of India) Act, 1990.

(b) "appointed date" means the date appointed under section 3;

(c) "Authority" means the Broadcasting Authority of India established under section 3;

(d) "basic service" means a tier of service, to which subscription is required for access to any other tier of service.

(e) "broadcasting service" means a service whereby signs or signals transmitted, whether or not encrypted, comprise—

(i) any programme capable of being received, or received and displayed, as visual images, whether moving or still; or

(ii) any sound programme for reception; or

(iii) any programme, being a combination of both visual image (whether moving or still) and sound for reception or reception and display,

by persons having equipment appropriate for receiving, or receiving and displaying, as the case may be, that service, irrespective of the means of delivery of that service;

(f) "cable television service" means a local delivery service without using MMDS and "cable television operator" shall be construed accordingly;

(g) "Chairperson" means the Chairperson of the Authority appointed under sub-section (*4*) of section 3;

(h) "channel" means a set of frequencies used for transmission of a programme;

(i) "decoder" means an equipment for decoding an encrypted channel or a compressed digital channel to facilitate its intelligible reception;

(j) "Doordarshan" shall have the same meaning as is assigned to it in clause (*h*) of section 2 of Prasar Bharati (Broadcasting Corporation of India) Act, 1990;

(k) "Direct-to-Home service" means a service which uses a Ku band satellite system for distribution of programmes direct to subscriber's premises without the help of a local delivery system;

(l) "encrypted" means treated electronically or otherwise for the purpose of preventing intelligible reception by unauthorised persons;

(m) "frequency" means frequency of electro-magnetic waves used for transmission of broadcasting service;

(n) "foreign satellite broadcasting service" means a satellite broadcasting service transmitted from a foreign country receivable in India;

(o) "free-to-air broadcasting service" means a broadcasting service made available for reception by broadcasting apparatus commonly available to the public without payment of a subscription fee;

(p) "foreign satellite system" means a satellite system other than Indian satellite system;

(q) "Indian satellite system" means a satellite system in an orbital slot allocated to India by the International Telecommunication Union;

(r) "licence" means a licence issued by the Authority under this Act;

(s) "licensed service" means a broadcasting service licensed by the Authority;

(t) "Local Delivery service" means a service for distribution of programmes by a ground transmission system using cable or MMDS or a combination of both to be called "Local Delivery System" for simultaneous reception by multiple subscribers;

(u) "Member" means a Part-time Member or an *ex officio* Member, as the case may be, of the Authority referred to in sub-section (*3*) of section 3 and includes the Chairperson;

(v) "MMDS" means a ground wireless transmission system used for multi-point multi-channel distribution of programmes on frequencies notified in the Official Gazette by the Wireless Advisor to the Government of India;

(w) "notification" means a notification published in the Official Gazette and the expression "notified" shall be construed accordingly;

(x) "permitted service" means a foreign satellite channel permitted by the Authority for reception in India;

(y) "prescribed" means prescribed by rules made under this Act;

(z) "private communication" means—

(i) a communication between two or more persons that is of a private or domestic nature;

(ii) an internal communication of a business, government agency or other organisation for the purpose of the operation of the business, agency or organisation; and

(iii) communications in such other circumstances as may be prescribed.

(za) "programme" in relation to a broadcasting service, means,—

(i) any matter the purpose of which is related to entertain, educate or inform public, or

(ii) any advertising or sponsorship matter, whether or not of a commercial kind;

but does not include any matter that is wholly related to or connected with any private communication.

(zb) "programme standard" means standard determined by the Authority relating to the content or delivery of programmes in respect of licensed services or permitted services;

(zc) "public service broadcaster" means any body created by an Act of Parliament for the purpose of public service broadcasting :

Provided that till the commencement of the Prasar Bharati Act, 1990, the public service broadcaster shall mean the All India Radio or the Doordarshan as the case may be;

(zd) "regulations" means regulations made by the Authority under this Act;

(ze) "satellite broadcasting service" means a service provided by using a satellite and received with or without the help of a local delivery system but does not include Direct-to-Home service;

(zf) "satellite radio broadcasting service" means a satellite broadcasting service for providing audio programmes;

(zg) "satellite television broadcasting service" means a satellite broadcasting service for providing video programmes with or without audio;

(zh) "Secretary-General" means the Secretary-General appointed under sub-section (*1*) of section 6;

(zi) "service provider" means provider of a broadcasting

service;

(zj) "station" means any broadcasting station with studios or transmitters or both and includes a relay station;

(zk) "subscriber" of a service means a person who receives the service at a place indicated by him without further transmitting it to any other person;

(zl) "subscription fee" means any form of consideration given by subscriber;

(zm) "terrestrial broadcasting service" means a service provided by using a ground transmitter but does not include a local delivery service;

(zn) "terrestrial radio broadcasting service" means a terrestrial broadcasting service for providing audio programmes;

(zo) "terrestrial television broadcasting service" means a terrestrial broadcasting service for providing video programme with or without audio;

(zp) "tier of service" means a category of Local Delivery service or Direct-to-Home service for which a separate rate is charged by the service provider;

(zq) "uplinking" with reference to satellite broadcast or Direct-to-Home service means uplinking of programme transmission from an earth station to the satellite;

(zr) "Wireless Adviser" means the Wireless Adviser to the Government of India;

(zs) "year" means the financial year.

CHAPTER II

THE BROADCASTING AUTHORITY OF INDIA

Establishment and composition of Authority

3. (*1*) With effect from such date as the Central Government may by notification appoint in this behalf, there shall be established for the purposes of this Act an Authority, to be known as the Broadcasting Authority of India.

(*2*) The Authority shall be a body corporate by the name aforesaid, having perpetual succession and a common seal with power to acquire, hold and dispose of property, both movable and immovable, and to contract, and shall by the said name sue and be sued.

(*3*) The Authority shall consist of the following Members, namely :

(a) a Chairperson;
(b) not more than eleven Part-time Members to be appointed by the Central Government in consultation with the Chairperson;
(c) Secretary to the Government of India incharge of Ministry of Information and Broadcasting, *ex officio*;
(d) Secretary to the Government of India incharge of Department of Telecommunications, *ex officio*;
(e) Secretary-General, *ex officio*.

(*4*) The Chairperson shall be appointed by the President of India on the recommendation of a Committee consisting of—

(a) the Chairman of the Council of States, who shall be the Chairman of the Committee;
(b) the Minister incharge of the Ministry of Information and Broadcasting to the Government of India; and
(c) the Chairman of the Press Council of India established under section 4 of the Press Council Act, 1978.

37 of 1978

(*5*) No appointment of a Member shall be invalidated merely by reason of any vacancy in, or any defect in the constitution of, the Committee appointed under sub-section (*4*).

(*6*) The Chairperson shall be appointed from amongst the persons of eminence with more than fifteen years of experience in one of the fields of administration, law, business management, broadcasting programme, broadcasting engineering, information management, journalism and communication.

(*7*) The Chairperson shall be a whole-time member and shall hold office for a term of five years from the date on which he enters upon his office or till he attains the age of sixty-five years, whichever is earlier and he shall not be eligible for reappointment.

(*8*) The Part-time Member shall be from amongst the persons of eminence in public life having knowledge or experience in one of the fields of education, literature, sports, culture, art, film, music, dramatics, broadcast programme, information management, communication, law, finance, administration, journalism, and business management.

(*9*) A Part-time Member shall hold office for a term of three years from the date on which he enters upon his office and he shall be eligible for reappointment for a second term.

(*10*) The salary and allowances payable to and other conditions of service of the Chairperson shall be such as may be prescribed.

(*11*) The allowances payable to the Part-time Members shall be such as may be prescribed.

(*12*) A person having any interest, direct or indirect, in any broadcasting agency shall not be eligible for appointment as Chairperson or a Part-time Member.

(*13*) No act or proceeding of the Authority shall be invalidated merely by reason of—

(a) any vacancy in, or any defect in the constitution of, the Authority or such committee; or

(b) any defect in the appointment of a person acting as a Member; or

(c) any irregularity in the procedure of the Authority not affecting the merits of the case.

Removal and suspension of Chairperson and Members

4. (*1*) The Chairperson or a Part-time Member may be removed or suspended from his office by the President in the manner and on grounds provided under article 317 of the Constitution of India for removal or suspension of the Chairperson or any other Member of the Union Public Service Commission :

Provided that a Part-time Member shall not be removed from his office on the ground that he is engaged during his term of office in any paid employment outside the duties of his office.

(*2*) The Chairperson or any other Part-time Member may resign his office by giving notice thereof in writing to the President of India and on such resignation being accepted, the Chairperson or other Member shall be deemed to have vacated his office.

Meeting of Authority

5. (*1*) The Authority shall meet at such times and places and shall observe such rules of procedure in regard to the transaction of business at its meetings as may be provided by regulations :

Provided that there shall not be less than eight meetings every year but two months shall not intervene between one meeting and the next meeting.

(*2*) The quorum at the meetings of the Authority shall be fifty per cent of the total number of Members.

(*3*) A Member shall be deemed to have vacated his office if he absents himself for three consecutive meetings of the Authority without the leave of the Chairperson.

(*4*) The Chairperson shall preside at the meetings of the Authority and if for any reason he is unable to attend any meeting, any other Member elected by the Members present at such meeting, shall preside at the meetings.

(*5*) All questions which come .up before any meeting of the Authority shall be decided by a majority of the votes of the Members present and voting and, in the event of an equality of votes, the Chairperson, or in his absence, the person presiding, shall have and exercise a second or casting vote.

Secretary-General of Authority and other officers

6. (*1*) The Central Government shall make available to the Authority, a panel of five officers of the rank of the Secretary to the Government of India and the Authority may appoint one of them as the Secretary-General of the Authority.

(*2*) The Secretary-General shall be the Chief Executive Officer of the Authority and shall exercise such powers and discharge such functions of the Authority as may be delegated to him by the Authority.

(*3*) The Authority may appoint such officers and other employees as it considers necessary for the efficient discharge of its functions under this Act in the manner as provided by the regulations.

(*4*) The salary and allowances payable to and other conditions of service of the officers and other employees of the Authority shall be such as may be determined by regulations.

CHAPTER III

FUNCTIONS OF AUTHORITY

Functions of Authority

7. (*1*) The functions of the Authority shall be—

(i) to carry out frequency planning of such frequencies or band of frequencies assigned to it by the wireless adviser to the Government of India for the purposes of broadcasting services;

(ii) to grant licences for broadcasting services;

(iii) to ensure that wide range of broadcasting services are available throughout India;

(iv) to ensure fair and effective competition in the provision of broadcasting services;

(v) to ensure the provision of services of high quality and offer a wide range of programmes to appeal to variety of tastes and interests;

(vi) to determine by regulations the programme code and standard;

(vii) to receive complaints for violation of code, provisions of this Act and rules and regulations made thereunder and for violation of conditions of licence and take such remedial measures as it considers necessary;

(viii) to consider and decide on fairness complaints referred to under sub-clause (i) and (ii) of clause (a) of sub-section (*2*);

(ix) to consider and decide standards complaints referred to under clause (b), (c) and (d) of sub-section (2);

(x) to set technical and other quality standards to ensure a reasonable quality of reception by means of regulations;

(xi) to perform such other functions as may be prescribed.

(2) The Authority may appoint a committee or committees of experts to advise on—

(a) practices to be followed in connection with the avoidance of —

(i) unjust and unfair treatment to any person in programmes;

(ii) unwarranted infringement of privacy in, or in connection with, obtaining of material included in such programmes;

(b) practices to be followed in connection with the portrayal of violence in programmes;

(c) practices to be followed in connection with the portrayal of sexual conduct in programmes;

(d) standards of taste and decency for programmes generally.

(3) The Authority may appoint a committee or committees of experts to monitor programmes and to make reports on the portrayal of violence and sexual conduct in and the standards of taste and decency observed in, such programmes generally and such report may include an assessment of either or both of the following, namely :

(i) the attitudes of the public at large towards the portrayal of violence or sexual conduct in, or towards the standards of taste and decency observed in, programmes; and

(ii) any effects or potential effects on the attitudes or behaviour of particular categories of persons of the portrayal of violence or sexual conduct in such programmes or of any failure to observe standards of taste and decency in such programmes.

CHAPTER IV

LICENCES

Prohibition on broadcasting service without licence

8. No person shall, after the commencement of this Act, provide any broadcasting service specified in sub-section (*1*) of section 9 without obtaining a licence in accordance with the provisions of this Act.

Licences to be granted by the Authority

9. (*1*) The Authority may grant licences for the following broadcasting services, namely :

(a) Terrestrial Radio Broadcasting;
(b) Terrestrial Television Broadcasting;
(c) Satellite Radio Broadcasting;
(d) Satellite Television Broadcasting;
(e) Direct to Home Broadcasting;
(f) Local Delivery Services;
(g) Such other services as may be prescribed.

(*2*) The Authority may further categorise the Terrestrial Broadcasting Services into analogue and digital and also into national, regional, local, restricted local services or any other similar service for the purposes of licences under this section and prevention of their accumulation under section 12.

(*3*) Nothing contained in this section shall apply to a public service broadcaster :

Provided that such public service broadcaster shall comply with all other provisions of this Act.

Conditions of licence

10 (*1*) The licence shall be granted subject to the following conditions, namely :

(i) that the licensee shall ensur that nothing is included in the programme of the licensee which offends against good taste or decency or is likely to encourage or incite to crime or to lead to disorder or to be offensive to public feeling;

(ii) that the licensee shall ensure that the news given in its programmes is presented with due accuracy and impartiality;

(iii) that the licensee shall ensure that due impartiality is maintained in respect of social or political issues of matter relating to public policy;

(iv) that the licensee shall ensure that due responsibility is exercised with respect to religious programmes with a view to avoiding—

(a) improper exploitation of religious susceptibilities; and

(b) offence to the religious views and beliefs of those belonging to a particular religion or religious denomination;

(v) that the licensee shall ensure that due emphasis is given in his programmes to promote values of national integration, religious harmony, scientific temper and Indian culture;

(vi) that the licensee shall ensure that such time, as may be determined by the Authority, is earmarked for broadcasting of—

(a) children's programmes, educational programmes, developmental programmes and programmes of Indian (regional or local) origin; and

(b) a range of diversity of independent production;

(vii) that the licensee shall follow the programme standards and codes set by the Authority;

(viii) that the licensee shall pay such licence fee in such manner as may be determined by the regulations;

(ix) that the licensee shall not carry out networking of local or regional broadcasting services without prior approval of the Authority;

(x) the Authority may vary the conditions of the licence by

giving to the licensee a reasonable opportunity of being heard; and

(xi) such other conditions as may be determined by the regulations.

(*2*) The licence granted for Direct-to-Home service or Local Delivery service shall be subject to the following conditions in addition to the conditions referred to in sub-section (*1*), namely :

(i) that the licensee shall provide a tier basic service which may include—

(a) a minimum number and type of terrestrial broadcasting services for every permitted service as determined by the regulations; and

(b) a minimum number and type of broadcasting services of the public service broadcaster as determined by the regulations;

(ii) that the licensee shall include only licensed services or permitted services in his delivery package for the purposes of distribution;

(iii) that the licensee shall use not more than such number of channels as determined by the regulations out of the total channels capacity of the system for providing his own programming :

Provided that such programmes as referred to in sub-clause (iii) above shall be subject to the programme standards and codes and such other conditions as may be required by the Authority for other broadcasting services.

Period of licence, etc.

11. (*1*) The period of licence for each category shall be for such period not exceeding ten years as may be determined by the regulations.

(*2*) A licence shall not be transferable.

(*3*) A licence shall lapse prior to its normal expiry in case of insolvency or death of the licensee.

Eligibility and restrictions for licences

12. (*1*) No person specified in Part I of the Schedule shall be eligible for the grant of a licence under this Act.

(*2*) No person shall be given the number of licences for a category of service more than the number prescribed for the category of service.

Explanation—For the purpose of this sub-section, the category of service shall be the same as referred to in section 9.

(*3*) No person shall be granted licence for more than one category of services specified in Part II of the Schedule.

(*4*) There shall be such restrictions on cross media ownership between the newspaper and broadcasting service as specified in Part III of the Schedule.

(*5*) The Central Government may, by notification in the Official Gazette, modify any limit on interest or equity holding in the body corporate or companies referred to in the Schedule.

(*6*) For the purposes of this section "person" includes connected persons referred to in paragraph 3 of Part IV of the Schedule.

Grant of licence for satellite broadcasting services

13. (*1*) Any person desirous of obtaining a satellite broadcasting licence shall apply to the Authority in such form as may be specified by the regulations.

(*2*) If the Authority is satisfied that the applicant—

(a) has acquired transponder either on an Indian satellite system or on a foreign satellite system;

(b) has obtained technical clearance in respect of the transponders, from the Wireless Adviser for the purposes of providing the proposed service; and

(c) has fulfilled all other conditions laid down under this Act and the rules and regulations made thereunder,

it may grant a licence to such person for satellite

broadcasting service on payment of such fee as may be determined by the regulations :

Provided that if the Authority refuses to grant the licence, it shall, before such refusal, give to the applicant an opportunity of being heard :

Provided further that a person providing a foreign satellite broadcasting service immediately before the commencement of this Act may continue to do so without a licence for a period of one month from such commencement, and if he has made an application for such licence under this Act within the said period of one month and such application is in the form and contains the particulars, as specified by the regulations, till the disposal of such application by the Authority.

Grant of licence for Direct-to-Home services

14. (*1*) The Authority shall invite bids for grant of licence for Direct-to-Home service and the licence shall be granted to the highest bidder if he fulfils all the conditions for the grant of such licence.

(*2*) The Authority shall grant such number of licences, not less than two, as may be prescribed.

Special provisions for satellite broadcasting and Direct-to-Home services

15. (*1*) For the purposes of sections 13 and 14, the Wireless Adviser shall—

(i) give technical clearance for licensing of satellite broadcasting services or Direct-to-Home Services on Indian satellite system or a foreign satellite system :

Provided that such clearance may be refused on technical or security considerations;

(ii) in cases where operations of the services are permitted with foreign satellite system, while giving technical clearance for relicensing or renewal of such services, give priority for their operations with Indian satellite system;

(2) The licensee shall carry out the uplinking of satellite broadcasting services or Direct-to-Home services from India only :

Provided that uplinking from outside the country may be permitted in respect of these services for coverage of live events taking place outside the country subject to such criteria as determined by the regulations :

Provided further that the Authority may also permit continuance of uplinking of satellite broadcasting services being received in India immediately before the commencement of this Act from outside the country till such time as it is reasonably required for shifting or creating the necessary uplinking facilities in India on payment of such additional licence fee as deemed fit.

Grant of licence for terrestrial broadcasting services

16. (*1*) The Authority shall invite bids for grant of licence for terrestrial broadcasting service and the licence shall be granted to the highest bidder if he fulfils all the conditions for the grant of such licence.

(*2*) Notwithstanding anything contained in sub-section (*1*), the Authority may grant licences to such institutions as may be notified for terrestrial broadcasting services through restricted bids or on payment of such licence fee as may be determined by the regulations :

Provided that no institution shall be notified under this sub-section unless the object of such institution is to provide education, community service, environment protection or health awareness:

Provided further that licence under this sub-section may be granted for such restricted area as may be determined by the regulations.

(*3*) The Wireless Adviser, shall assign to the Authority for the purpose of grant of terrestrial broadcasting service licence such frequencies or band of frequencies as it may determine in consultation with the Authority.

Grant of licence for Local Delivery services

17. (*1*) The Authority shall grant two licences for Local Delivery service for each telecom circle as identified by the Central Government :

Provided that the Authority on technical or administrative grounds may restrict or widen a telecom circle for the purposes of this sub-section.

(*2*) The Authority shall invite bids for grant of licence for Local Delivery service and the licence shall be granted to the highest bidder if he fulfils all the conditions for the grant of such licence.

(*3*) The Wireless Adviser after consulting the Authority, shall assign frequencies for MMDS for providing Local Delivery service, wherever it is required.

(*4*) The Authority shall exempt the non-commercial establishments under common ownership from obtaining a licence for the purpose of providing cable television services for the exclusive use of their members.

(*5*) The Central Government, may, by notification confer upon any licensee of the local delivery services, such rights and obligations, as it may consider necessary, in respect of placing and maintaining of his cable networks as available to the telegraph authority under Part-III of the Indian Telegraph Act, 1885.

13 of 1885

Enforcement of licences

18. (*1*) The Authority may take following actions in case of breach of any terms of the licence, after providing an opportunity to the licensee of being heard, namely :

(a) direct licensee to broadcast correction or apology or not to repeat a programme; or

(b) to impose a penalty, which may extend up to rupees fifty lakhs; or

(c) suspend the licence for a specified period; or

(d) curtail the period of the licence; or

(e) revoke the licence.

(*2*) An aggrieved person may prefer an appeal against an action of the Authority in High Court having jurisdiction within thirty days of such action.

Explanation—For the purpose of this sub-section, "High Court having jurisdiction" means the High Court within the jurisdiction of which the aggrieved person ordinarily resides or carries on business or personally works for gain relating to the subject matter of the action against which the appeal is preferred.

CHAPTER V

FINANCE, ACCOUNTS AND AUDIT

Funds, accounts, budget and audit of the Authority

19. (*1*) The proceeds of the licence fee shall be credited to the Consolidated Fund of India.

(*2*) The Central Government may for enabling the Authority to discharge it's functions efficiently, after due appropriation made by Parliament by law in this behalf, pay to the Authority in each financial year such sums of money as the Government considers necessary by way of grants-in-aid.

(*3*) The Authority shall have its own fund and all the receipts of the Authority shall be credited to the fund and all payments by the Authority shall be made therefrom. All money belonging to the fund shall be deposited in one or more Nationalised Banks in such manner as the Authority may decide and Authority may spend such sums as it thinks fit for performing its function under this Act.

(*4*) The Authority shall prepare, in such form and at such time each year as may be prescribed, a budget in respect of the financial year next ensuing showing—

(a) the expenditure which is proposed to be met from the internal resources of the Authority; and

(b) the sums required from the Central Government to meet other expenses,

and copies thereof shall be forwarded to the Central Government.

(5) The Authority shall maintain proper accounts and other relevant records and prepare an annual statement of accounts in such form and in such manner as may be prescribed.

(*6*) The accounts of the Authority shall be audited by the Comptroller and Auditor-General of India at such intervals as may be specified by him and any expenditure incurred in connection with such audit shall be payable by the Authority to the Comptroller and Auditor-General.

(*7*) The Comptroller and Auditor-General of India and any person appointed by him in connection with the audit of the accounts of the Authority shall have the same rights and privileges and authority in connection with such audit as the Comptroller and Auditor-General has in connection with the audit of Government accounts and, in particular, shall have the right to demand the production of books, accounts, connected vouchers and other documents and papers and to inspect any of the offices of the Authority.

(*8*) The accounts of the Authority as certified by the Comptroller and Auditor-General of India or any other person appointed by him in this behalf together with the audit report thereon shall be forwarded annually to the Central Government and that Government shall cause the same to be laid before each House of Parliament.

20. (*1*) The Authority, after the end of each financial year, shall submit to the Central Government a report on their activities during the preceding financial year and containing such information relating to the proceedings and policy of the Authority, as the Government may prescribe from time to time.

(*2*) The Central Government shall cause such report to be laid before each House of Parliament.

CHAPTER VI

MISCELLANEOUS

Offence and punishment

21. A person who in contravention of the provisions of this Act, provides, distributes or receives any broadcasting service which is neither a licensed service nor a permitted service or abets or assists transmission of such service in any manner which may include collection of subscription for his principal, issuing of advertisements to such service, dealing in or distribution of decoders or dish antennas, shall be guilty of committing an offence of illegal broadcasting and on conviction, shall be punishable with imprisonment which may extend upto five years, or with fine which may extend upto rupees ten lakhs and in subsequent offence such fine may extend to rupees fifty lakhs, or with both.

Special provision for certain foreign satellite broadcasting services

22. Notwithstanding anything contained in this Act, the Authority, after receiving a request in this regard, may grant permission for reception of an unlicensed foreign satellite broadcasting service in India, if such a broadcasting service—

(i) is a free to air broadcasting service;
(ii) (a) does not carry any advertisements; or
(b) carries advertisements, for such duration as may be fixed by the Authority, and the service is devoted solely to sports or international news and current affairs; and
(iii) fulfils the programme standard with respect to permitted service :

Provided that the Authority may revoke such permission, if it is of the opinion that the service has contravened any of the conditions referred to above.

Prohibition of exclusive rights for live broadcasting of certain events

23. (*1*) No licensee shall carry a live broadcast of any sporting or other event of national or international interest, held in India, as may be specified by the regulations, without the consent of the Authority unless the public service broadcasters have also been given the broadcasting right for carrying the same.

(2) Any contract of exclusive broadcasting right of any event referred to in sub-section (*1*) above without the consent of the Authority, shall be void and inoperative.

Procedure and powers of the Authority

5 of 1908

24. (*1*) The Authority shall not be bound by the procedure laid down by the Code of Civil Procedure, 1908, but shall be guided by the principles of natural justice and, subject to the other provisions of this Act and of any rules, the Authority shall have powers to regulate its own procedure including the fixing of places and times of its enquiry.

(*2*) The Authority shall have, for the purposes of discharging its functions under this Act, the same powers as are vested in a civil court under the Code of Civil Procedure, 1908, while trying a suit, in respect of the following matters, namely :

(a) summoning and enforcing the attendance of any person and examining him on oath;
(b) requiring the discovery and production of documents;
(c) receiving evidence on affidavits;
(d) issuing commissions for the examination of witnesses or documents;
(e) any other matter which may be prescribed.

Powers of the Central Government

25. (*1*) In the event of war or a natural calamity of national magnitude, the Central Government may, in public interest, take over the control and management of any broadcasting

service or any facility connected therewith, suspend its operation or entrust the public service broadcaster to manage it in the manner directed by the government for such period as it deems fit.

(*2*) The Central Government may if it appears necessary or expedient to do so, may, in public interest, at any time require the Authority to direct any licensee to—

(a) transmit in his broadcasting service such announcements in such a manner as may be considered necessary;

(b) stop any broadcasting service which is considered prejudicial to friendly relations with a foreign country, public order, security of state, or communal harmony.

(*3*) The Central Government may, in public interest, issue such other directions, to the Authority, from time to time as considered necessary.

Powers of the Authority, information, conduct enquiries, take evidence, etc.

26. (*1*) The licensee shall commence operation of his service within such period as may be specified by the Authority and maintain such documentary records and transmission schedules as may be specified by the regulations and allow inspections of records authorised by the Authority.

(*2*) The Authority may call for any information from the licensee which is necessary for transparency and ascertaining the true ownership of the licensee.

(*3*) The Authority may give directions to the licensee as it considers necessary in public interest.

(*4*) The Authority or any officer authorised by the Authority shall have power to inspect and obtain information, wherever necessary, from programme producers, distributors and advertising agents.

1 of 1956

(*5*) For effective enforcement of restrictions on holding of licences, as provided under section 12, the Authority or any officer authorised by the Authority for that purpose, shall have all the powers of an inspecting officer as provided under Section 209-A of the Companies Act, 1956.

(*6*) It shall be the duty of every licensee to carry out the directions of the Authority given under this section.

(*7*) If default is made by a licensee in complying with the provisions of sub-section (*6*), the Authority may cancel the licence of the concerned person after providing him an opportunity of being heard.

Chairperson, members, etc. to be public servants

27. Every member, every officer or other employee of the Authority and every member of a Committee thereof, shall be deemed to be a public servant within the meaning of section 21 of the Indian Penal Code.

Protection of action taken in good faith

28. No suit or other legal proceeding shall lie against the Authority, any member or officer or other employee thereof for anything which is in, good faith done or intended to be done in pursuance of this Act or of any rules or regulations made thereunder.

Delegation of powers

29. The Authority may by general or special order, delegate to the of Chairperson or any other Member or to any officer of the Authority, subject to such conditions and limitations, if any, as may be specified therein, such of its powers and duties under this Act as it may deem fit.

Application of other laws not barred

30. (*1*) The provisions of this Act shall be in addition to, and not in derogation of the provisions of any other law for the time being in force.

(*2*) Notwithstanding anything contained in sub-section (*1*), where any Act or omission constitutes an offence punishable under this Act and also under any other Act, then the offender found guilty of such offence, shall punished under this Act and not under the other Act.

Power to make rules

31. (*1*) The Central Government may, by notification, make rules for carrying out provisions of this Act.

(*2*) In particular and without prejudice to the generality of the foregoing power, such rules may provide for all or any of the following matters, namely :

(a) to provide other circumstances for communication under sub-clause (iii) of clause (z) of section 2;

(b) the salaries and allowances payable and other conditions of service of the Chairperson under sub-section (*10*) of section 3;

(c) the allowances payable to the Part-time Members under sub-section (*11*) of section 3;

(d) the other functions to be performed by the Authority under clause (xi) of sub-section (*1*) of section 7;

(e) the other services under clause (g) of sub-section (*1*) of section 9;

(f) the number for the category of service more than which the licence cannot be given to a person under sub-section (*2*) of section 12;

(g) the number of licences to be granted by the Authority under sub-section (*2*) of section 14;

(h) the form in which and the time at which in each year the Authority shall prepare a budget under sub-section (*4*) of section 19;

(i) the form and the manner in which the annual statement of accounts shall be prepared under sub-section (*5*) of section 19;

(j) the information relating to the proceedings and policy of the Authority to be contained in a report to be submitted by the Authority under sub-section (*1*) of section 20;

(k) any other matter regarding which the Authority shall have the powers of civil court under clause (e) of sub-section (*2*) of section 24;

(l) any other matter which is required to be, or may be prescribed.

Power to make regulations

32. (*1*) The Authority may, by notification, make regulations not inconsistent with this Act and the rules made thereunder for enabling it to perform its functions under this Act.

(*2*) Without prejudice to the generality of the foregoing power such regulations may provide for all or any of the following matters, namely :

(a) the times and places at which meetings of the Authority shall be held and, the procedure to be followed thereat, and the procedure in regard to the transaction of the business at a meeting of the Authority under sub-section (*1*) of section 5;

(b) the manner of appointment of officers and other employees of the Authority under sub-section (*3*) of section 6;

(c) the salary and allowances payable to and other conditions of service of the officers and other employees of the Authority under sub-section (*4*) of section 6;

(d) the programme code and standards to be determined under clause (vi) of sub-section (*1*) of section 7;

(e) the reasonable quality of reception under clause (f) of sub-section (*1*) of section 7;

(f) the manner in which the licence fee shall be paid by the licensee under clause (viii) of sub-section (*1*) of section 10;

(g) the other conditions under clause (xi) of sub-section (*1*) of section 10, subject to which the licence shall be granted;

(h) the minimum number and type of terrestrial broadcasting services for every permitted service under sub-clause (a) of clause (i) of sub-section (*2*) of section 10;

(i) the minimum number and type of broadcasting services of the public service broadcaster under sub-clause (b) of clause (i) of sub-section (*2*) of section 10;

(j) the number of channels to be used by the licensee under

clause (iii) of sub-section (*2*) of section 10;

(k) the period of licence for each category under sub-section (*1*) of section 11;

(l) the form in which any person desirous of obtaining a satellite broadcasting licence shall apply to the Authority under sub-section (*1*) of section 13;

(m) the fee payable for grant of a licence to the applicant for satellite broadcasting service under sub-section (*2*) of section 13;

(n) the form of application and the particulars to be contained therein under second proviso to clause (c) of sub-section (*2*) of section 13;

(o) the criteria subject to which the uplinking from outside the country may be permitted in respect of these services for coverage of live events taking place outside the country under first proviso to caluse (iii) of sub-section (*3*) of section 15;

(p) the licence fee to be paid for grant of licences to the institutions under sub-section (*2*) of section 16;

(q) the restricted area for which licence may be granted under second proviso to sub-section (*2*) of section 16;

(r) any sporting or other event of national or international interest, of which a live broadcast shall be carried out by the licensee without the consent of the Authority under sub-section (*1*) of section 23;

(s) the documentary record and transmission schedule to be maintained by the licensee under sub-section (*1*) of section 26;

(t) the conditions of licence to be granted under sub-section (*4*) of section 35;

(p) any other matter in respect of which provision is, in the opinion of the Authority, necessary for the performance of its functions under this Act.

Rules and regulations to be laid before Parliament

33. Every rule and every regulation made under this Act shall be laid, as soon as may be after it is made, before each House of Parliament, while it is in session for a total period of thirty days which may be comprised in one session or in

two or more successive sessions, and if, before the expiry of the session immediately following the session or the successive sessions aforesaid, both Houses agree in making any modification in, the rule or regulation, or both Houses agree that the rule or regulation should not be made, the rule or regulation shall thereafter have effect only in such modified form or be of no effect, as the case may be; so, however, that any such modification or annulment shall be without prejudice to the validity of anything previously done under that rule or regulation.

Power to remove difficulties

34. (*1*) If any difficulty arises in giving effect to the provisions of this Act, the Central Government may, by order published in the Official Gazette, make such provisions, not inconsistent with the provisions of this Act, as it may deem necessary, for the removal of the difficulty :

Provided that no such order shall be made after the expiry of a period of three years from the commencement of this Act.

(*2*) Every order made under this section shall be laid, as soon as may be, after it is made, before each House of Parliament.

Repeal and saving

35. (*1*) The Cable Television Networks (Regulation) Act, 1995 is hereby repealed.

(*2*) Notwithstanding such repeal any cable network registered under that Act may continue to provide cable services if the cable operator providing service has made an application to the Authority for the grant of a licence under this section within six months from the date of the commencement of this Act or where he has made such an application till the disposal of such application which ever is later.

(*3*) The Authority may, on receipt of an application under sub-section (*2*) grant or refuse to grant a licence for providing cable services :

Provided that no such licence shall be granted to any cable television network which provides such service to more than five thousand households and from more than one location :

Provided further that no application shall be refused under this sub-section unless the applicant has been given a reasonable opportunity of presenting his case.

(*4*) A licence granted under this section shall be subject to such conditions as may be determined by the regulations.

(*5*) Save as provided in this section no person shall provide any cable services after the commencement of this Act.

(*6*) The Authority shall for regulating the cable networks under this section authorise the concerned district magistrates or sub-divisional magistrate to receive public complaints, give notice to the operators, make such enquiries and take such evidence as considered necessary and forward the report to the Authority and on the basis of such report, if the Authority feels that there is sufficient reason to do so, it may take such action as it deems fit under sub-section (*1*) of section 18.

THE SCHEDULE

(*See* Section 12)

RESTRICTIONS ON THE HOLDING OF LICENCES

PART 1

Disqualification for Holding of Licences

The following persons shall be disqualified for the purposes of grant of licence under this Act.

General disqualification

1. (a) An individual who is not an Indian national;
   (b) A partnership firm all of whose partners are not citizens of India;

(c) Companies not incorporated in India;
(d) Companies incorporated in India but with.

(i) foreign equity in case of terrestrial broadcast services;
(ii) foreign equity exceeding 49% in case of other services not mentioned in (i) above and management control not with the Indian shareholders.

(e) Governments and local authorities;
(f) Any person convicted of an offence under this Act or convicted of the offences referred to in section 8 of the Representation of the People Act, 1951 (43 of 1951) or declared as insolvent;
(g) A body, which is controlled by a person, referred to in any of clauses (a) to (e) above; and
(h) A body corporate, in which a body referred to in clause (g) above, is a participant with more than a 5 per cent interest.

Explanation—"Foreign equity" for the purposes of this Part, shall be notified by the Central Government, from time to time.

2. Disqualification of religious bodies.

(a) a body whose objectives are wholly or mainly of a religious nature;
(b) a body which is controlled by a body referred to in clause (a) or by two or more such bodies taken together.
(c) a body which controls a body referred to in clause (a);
(d) a body corporate which is associate of a body corporate referred to in clause (a), (b) or (c);
(e) a body corporate in which a body referred to in any of clauses (a) to (d) is a participant with more than five per cent interest;
(f) an individual who is an officer of a body referred to in clause (a); and
(g) a body which is controlled by an individual referred to in clause (f) or by two or more such individuals taken together.

3. Disqualification of political bodies.

(a) a body whose objects are wholly or mainly of a political nature;
(b) a body affiliated to a body, referred to in clause (a);
(c) an individual who is an officer of a body, referred to in clause (a) or (b);
(d) a body corporate, which is an associate of a body corporate referred to in clause (a) or (b);
(e) a body corporate in which a body referred to in any of clauses (a) and (b) is a participant with more than a five per cent interest;
(f) a body which is controlled by a person referred to in any of clauses (a) to (d) or by two or more persons, taken together;
(g) a body corporate, in which a body referred to in clause (f), other than one which is controlled by a person, referred to in clause (c) or by two or more such persons, taken together, is a participant with more than a five per cent interest.

4. Disqualification of publicly funded bodies.

(a) a body (other than a local authority) which has in its last financial year received more than half its income from public funds;
(b) a body which is controlled by a body referred to in clause (a) or by two or more such bodies taken together; and
(c) a body corporate in which a body referred to in clause (a) or (b) is participant with more than a five per cent interest.

5. Disqualification of advertising agencies.

(a) an advertising agency;
(b) an associate of an advertising agency;
(c) any body which is controlled by a person referred to in sub-clause (a) or by two or more such persons taken together; and
(d) any body corporate in which a person referred to in any of sub-clauses (a) to (c) is a participant with more than a five per cent interest.

PART II

RESTRICTIONS TO PREVENT ACCUMULATION OF INTEREST IN LICENSED SERVICES

1. A person shall be allowed to hold licences in only one of the following category of services :

   (a) Terrestrial radio broadcasting;
   (b) Terrestrial television broadcasting;
   (c) Satellite television or radio broadcasting;
   (d) Diret-to-Home broadcasting;
   (e) Local delivery services;
   (f) Any other category or categories of service(s) which may be notified by the Central Government for the purpose.

2. Any restriction on participation imposed as above on the holder of a licence shall apply to him as if he and every person connected with him were one person.

PART III

RESTRICTIONS ON CONTROLLING INTEREST IN BOTH NEWSPAPERS AND LICENSED SERVICES

1.1 No proprietor of a newspaper shall either be a participant with more than twenty per cent interest in or control a body corporate which is the holder of a licence to provide a licensed service under this Act.

1.2 No proprietor of a newspaper, who is a participant with more than five but less than twenty per cent interest, in a body corporate and not controlling such a body corporate, holding a licence shall be a participant with more than a five per cent interest in any other such body corporate.

1.3 No person who is the holder of a licence to provide licensed service under this Act shall be either a participant with more than twenty per cent interest in or control a body corporate which controls a newspaper.

1.4 No person who is the holder of a licence and is a participant with more than five but less than twenty per cent interest in a body corporate and not controlling such a body corporate which runs a national newspaper, shall be a participant with more than five per cent interest in any other such body corporate.

2. For the purposes of this Part, a person controls a newspaper if—

(a) he is the proprietor of such a newspaper; or
(b) he controls a body which is the proprietor of such a newspaper.

3. Any restriction on participation imposed as above on the proprietor of any newspaper or on the holder of licence shall apply to him as if he and every person connected with him were one person.

PART IV

1. (*1*) For the purposes of this Schedule—

"Advertising Agency" means an individual or a body corporate who carries on business as an advertising agent (whether individual or in partnership) or has control over any body corporate which carries on business as an advertising agent, and any reference to an advertising agency includes reference to an individual who —

(a) is a director or officer of any body corporate which carries on such a business, or
(b) is employed by any person who carries on such a business;

"Associate"—

(a) in relation to a body corporate, means a director of that body corporate or a body corporate inter connected with that body corporate;
(b) in relation to the partner of a firm, means a relative of such partner and includes any other partner of such firm;

(c) in relation to the trustee of a trust, means any other trustee of such trust;

(d) in relation to an individual, shall be construed in accordance with sub-clause (3); and

(e) where a person or a body corporate is an associate of another person or body corporate, the latter shall also be deemed to be an associate of the former.

"Control"—

(a) in relation to a body corporate, shall be construed in accordance with sub-clause (3), and

(b) in relation to any body other than a body corporate, means the power of a person to secure, by virtue of the rules regulating that or any other body, that the affairs of the first-mentioned body are conducted in accordance with the wishes of that person,

and would include control as a result of, or by means of, trusts, agreements, arrangements, understandings and practices, whether or not having legal or equitable force and whether or not based on legal or equitable rights.

"Newspaper" means as defined under the Press and Registration of Books Act, 1867 (25 of 1867).

(*2*) For the purpose of determining the persons who are an individual's associates for the purposes of this Schedule, the following persons shall be regarded as associates of each other, namely :

(a) any individual and that individual's husband or wife and any relative, or husband or wife of a relative, of that individual or of that individual's husband or wife;

(b) any individual and any body corporate of which that individual is a director;

(c) any person in his capacity as trustee of a settlement and the settlor or grantor and any person associated with the settlor or grantor;

(d) persons carrying on business in partnership and the

husband or wife and relatives of any of them;

(e) any two or more persons acting together to secure or exercise control of a body corporate or other association or to secure control of any enterprise or assets;

and in this sub-paragraph "relative" means as defined under the Companies Act, 1956.

(*3*) A person controls a body corporate if —

(a) he has a controlling interest in the body, or

(b) (although not having such an interest in the body) he is able, by virtue of the holding of shares or the possession of voting power in or in relation to the body or any other body corporate, to secure that the affairs of the body are conducted in accordance with his wishes, or

(c) he has the power, by virtue of any powers conferred by the articles of association or other document regulating the body or any other body corporate, to secure that the affairs of the body are so conducted,

and tor this purpose, in the absence of proof to the contrary, a person has a controlling interest in a body corporate if he holds, or is beneficially entitled to, more than twenty per cent of the equity share capital in that body, or possesses more than twenty per cent of the voting power in it.

(*4*) It is hereby declared that a person may be regarded as controlling a body corporate by virtue of clause (b) of sub-clause (3) despite the fact that—

(a) he does not have a controlling interest in any such other body corporate as is mentioned in that paragraph, or

(b) any such other body corporate does not have a controlling interest in the body in question, or

(c) he and any such other body corporate together do not have a controlling interest in that body.

(*5*) For the purposes of any provision of this Schedule which refers to a body controlled by two or more persons or bodies of any description taken together, the persons or bodies in question shall not be regarded as controlling the body by virtue of paragraph (b) of sub-paragraph (3) unless thay are acting together in concert.

(6) In this Schedule any reference to a participant with more than a five per cent or, as the case may be, twenty per cent interest in a body corporate is a reference to a person who—

(a) holds or is beneficially entitled to more than five or, as the case may be, twenty per cent of the shares in that body, or

(b) possesses more than five or, as the case may be, twenty per cent of the voting power in that body,

and, where any such reference has been amended by an order under this Schedule varying the percentage in question, this sub-paragraph shall have effect in relation to it subject to the necessary modifications.

2. (*1*) Any reference in paragraph 1 to a person—

(a) holding or being entitled to shares, or any amount of the shares or equity share capital, in a body corporate, or

(b) possessing voting power, or any amount of the voting power, in a body corporate,

is a reference to his doing so, or being so entitled, whether alone or jointly with one or more other persons and whether directly or through one or more nominees.

(*2*) "Inter connected Undertakings or Corporate Bodies" shall have the same meaning as assigned in the Monopolies and Restrictive Trade Practices Act, 1969 (54 of 1969).

(*3*) For the purposes of this Schedule, the following persons are connected with each other in relation to a particular licence, namely :

(a) the licence holder;

(b) a person who controls the licence holder;

(c) an associate of the licence holder or of a person referred to in clause (b); and

(d) a body which is controlled by the licence holder or by an associate of the licence holder.

STATEMENT OF OBJECTS AND REASONS

The broadcasting scenario, especially in the realm of satellite broadcasting, has undergone a revolution during the last few years. A large number of satellite television channels have been beaming their programmes through the Indian skies to our people. All these channels are foreign entities and their programmes are uplinked from outside the country without any regulation through the law of our land, while Indian entrepreneurs and Indian companies are not at present permitted to own either Radio or Television stations.

2. Concern has been voiced both inside Parliament and outside about the implications of these unregulated television programmes and the denial of level playing field to Indian entities. The only legal instrument available is the Indian Telegraph Act, 1885, which is considered totally inadequate to govern modern broadcasting media. All leading democratic countries have enacted laws specifically regulating broadcasting media. The introduction of the Broadcasting Bill is a step in this direction.

3. It is felt that the public service broadcaster alone will not be able to meet the needs and urges of the people in terms of variety and plurality of programmes required in different regions by different sections of society in our vast country. Keeping in view our great democratic traditions, it is imperative that our citizens are well informed and given wider choice in matters of information, education and entertainment. This can be provided by facilitating private broadcasting in the country.

4. The Bill seeks to establish an autonomous Broadcasting Authority for the purposes of facilitating and regulating broadcasting services in India so that they become competitive in terms of quality of services, cost of service and use of new technologies, apart from becoming a catalyst for social change, promotion of values of Indian culture and shaping of a modern vision. It will also curb monopolistic trends in this sensitive field, so that people are provided with a wide range of news and views.

The Bill seeks to achieve the said objectives.

NEW DELHI;
The 12th May, 1997 S. JAIPAL REDDY

NOTES ON CLAUSES

Clause 2 defines the various expressions occurring in the Bill.

Clause 3 provides for the establishment of the Broadcasting Authority of India.

Clause 4 provides that the President may on the grounds provided under article 317 of the Constitution remove or suspend the Chairperson and Members.

Clause 5 provides detailed provisions regarding the conduct of the meetings of the Authority.

Clause 6 provides procedure for appointment of Secretary-General of Authority and empowers the Authority to appoint other officers.

Clause 7 provides functions of the Authority and empowers the Authority to appoint committees of experts to advise on matters considered necessary.

Clause 8 provides prohibition on broadcasting service without license by any person.

Clause 9 specifies the different services for which licences may be granted by the Authority.

Clause 10 specifies the conditions for granting licences for broadcasting services licences.

Clause 11 provides for the period of broadcasting licence and other conditions.

Clause 12 specifies the eligibility and restrictions for licences to be granted by the Authority.

Clause 13 gives procedure for grant of licence for satellite broadcasting services.

Clause 14 provides procedure for grant of licence for Direct-to-Home services.

Clause 15 provides for special provisions for satellite broadcasting and Direct-to-Home services.

Clause 16 provides procedure for grant of licence for terrestrial broadcasting services.

Clause 17 provides procedure for grant of licence for local delivery services by the Authority.

Clause 18 gives the details of actions which can be taken by the Authority for enforcement of licences.

Clause 19 provides that licence fee shall be credited to the Consolidated Fund of India and also specifies the maintenance of the accounts, budget and audit by the Comptroller-Auditor-General of India by the Authority.

Clause 20 provides for furnishing of the Annual Report to the Central Government which shall be laid before the Parliament.

Clause 21 prescribes offence and punishment.

Clause 22 provides special provisions for certain foreign satellite broadcasting services.

Clause 23 empowers the Authority to refuse licence for live broadcasting of certain events of national and international importance.

Clause 24 enumerates the procedure and powers of the Authority.

Clause 25 specifies the powers of the Central Government in event of war or natural calamities.

Clause 26 provides powers of the Authority to seek information, conduct enquiries, take evidence, for operation and regulation licences and also empowers the Authority to give directions to licences.

Clause 27 provides that Chairperson and Members of the Authority shall be deemed to be a public servant within the meaning of section 21 of the Indian Penal Code.

Clause 28 provides for usual provisions relating to the protection of action taken in good faith by the Authority or Chairperson or Members or officers and other employees of the Authority.

Clause 29 provides for delegation of powers of the Authority to Chairperson or other Member or other officers.

Clause 30 provides that application of other laws are not barred and in case of an offence committed under this Act and also under another Act, the offender shall be punished under this Act.

Clause 31 confers on the Central Government powers to make rules for carrying out the provisions of the Bill.

Clause 32 confers on the Authority the powers to make regulation consistent with provision of this Bill and rules made by the Central Government thereunder before each House of Parliament.

Clause 33 provides laying of the rules and regulations before Parliament.

Clause 34 empowers the Central Government to remove difficulties which may arise in giving effect to the provisions of the Bill.

Clause 35 provides for repeal of the Cable Television Networks

(Regulation) Act, 1995 and for licensing and regulations of cable networks registered under that Act on the date of commencement of this Act.

FINANCIAL MEMORANDUM

The Central Government proposes to set up an independent statutory Broadcast Authority under clause 3 of the Bill. Recurring expenditure towards pay and allowances, etc., of the Chairperson and other members under sub-clauses (10) and (11) of clause 3 will be of the order of Rs. 30 lakhs per annum and of the officers and employees of the Authority under sub-clause (4) of clause 6 will be of the order of rupees 2 crores per annum. Non-recurring expenditure by way of purchase of accommodation, furniture and fixtures, office equipment, vehicle, etc. will be approximately of the order of rupees 10 crores.

LIST OF CONTRIBUTORS

Vir Bala Aggarwal is currently Reader in the Department of Journalism and Mass Communication, Himachal Pradesh University, Shimla. She has contributed a number of research and popular papers to academic journals, seminars and conferences. She has been frequently writing on Media, Development and Women Issues. With Prof. V. S. Gupta, she has published *Media Policy and Nation Building—Select Issues and Themes.*

Ajit Bhattacharjea, currently Director, Press Institute of India, New Delhi, is a veteran journalist and a well known columnist. He joined the profession before independence and has been the Editor of the *Hindustan Times*. Presently he is working for the passage of the Right to Information Bill.

D. K. Bose, currently working with the Media Division of R.K. Swamy/BBDO Advertising Ltd., has over 32 years experience in Advertising and Communication Management with a specialisation in Media Planning, Media Research and Development. He has also worked as the Head of Media Functions in three Prestigious multinational advertising agencies such as C & M, HTA for 17 years.

Vijayluxmi Bose is currently a senior Faculty Member at the Mass Communication Research Centre, Jamia Millia Islamia, New Delhi. A researcher by training in the area of health communication, educational technology and informatics, she has been the Project Leader of the LPDC/UNESCO and IDRC sponsored course for the training of Communication Field Researchers at MCRC, JMI.

Melissa Butcher is currently Ph.D. Scholar, International Communications Programme, Macquarie University, Sydney, Australia.

Rajeshwar Dyal is currently working as Media Advisor with Friedrich-Ebert-Foundation, which aims at democratisation and pluralism in media, organising media activities with media in the government and private sector, academia from various departments and other research institutions. He was with the Indian Institute of Mass Communication, New Delhi for 15 years prior to joining the present assignment in 1992. He has an experience of more than 20 years in communication research and training and interaction with national and international media organisations and activities. With Prof. V. S. Gupta, he has edited *Rural Press—Problems and Prospects, and National Media Policy.*

P. P. Ghosh is currently the Director of the Asian Development Research Institute (ADRI), Patna. Most of his research writings are on the issues of rural development and regional planning; of late, he has been working on the issue of macroeconomic policy changes in the Indian economy particularly its impact on human resource development. He has two books, several research reports and about thirty research articles to his credit.

V. S. Gupta, currently Professor at Haryana Agricultural University, was awarded the UNDP Fellowship for training in Europe and selected for the Journalist Fellowship Award for working in the area of Environment and Development. He conceptualised and implemented as Course Director the Post-Graduate Diploma in Agricultural Journalism and Refresher Course in Communication and Writing Skills in the university. He has written and edited over half a dozen books including *Media and Development, Third Revolution in Indian Perspective, National Media Policy*, and *Media Policy and Nation Building*, singly and jointly. He is the Country Representative for the Asian Media Information and Communication Centre (AMIC), Singapore. His forthcoming book is *Communication Technology, Media Policy and National Development—An Indian Perspective.*

B. S. Hansra is presently working as Assistant Director General (Agri. Extension) with Indian Council of Agricultural Research, New Delhi. Prior to joining ICAR, Dr. Hansra worked as Professor and Head, Department of Extension Education, Punjab Agricultural University, Ludhiana (Punjab). He has more than 180 publications including ten books. Dr. Hansra has been nominated as an International Union of Forestry Research Organisation Officer for 1996-2000.

S. Kasbekar is currently, Head, School of Journalism & Mass Communication, Devi Ahilya University, Indore. She has conducted research in the areas of Mass Communication and Development Communication. She is on the Advisory Board of Akashvani, Indore and Doordarshan, Bhopal, and also Honorary Editor of *Indore Manager* (AIMA) and *Prayog*.

Frank Krishner is Communication Expert, Alternate Media, Patna.

K. P. Madhu is currently Joint Director (Software) at the Consortium for Educational Communication, an apex body for Countrywide Classroom Programmes of the UGC. He has made many programmes in the area of science and technology. He was earlier the Executive Producer of the 'Turning Point' programme for Times Television.

Vijay Menon has been Secretary-General of the Asian Media Information and Communication Centre, a regional non-profit organisation, since 1982. He is concurrently Editor-in-Chief of the quarterly journal, *Media Asia* and the bi-monthly, *Asian Mass Communication Bulletin (AMCB).* Prior to joining AMIC, he was General Manager-India of a multinational advertising agency. He was also a visiting lecturer at the University of Bombay's J.B. Institute of Management Studies. Mr. Menon has been associated with various international and regional organisations including the Commonwealth Association for Education in Journalism and Communication (CAEJAC), UNESCO's International Network of Documentation Centres on Communication Research and Policy (COMENT); the International Institute of Communications (IIC), London, Pacific Communication Research Council, San Diego, USA, and the Commission on Education and Communications of IUCN). He has co-edited a book—*Passing of Remoteness*, Information Revolution in the Asia-Pacific and authored many papers on communication topics.

Gopal Misra currently working as a Policy Consultant for a renowned media group, SPA headed by Siddhartha Ray, is a free-lance journalist and a prolific writer. He writes for many Indian and foreign dailies such as the *Tribune* and the *Gulf News*, Dubai. During his nearly two-and-a half decades of Professional experience, he has worked in various newspapers, periodicals and weeklies, including the *Times of India, Pioneer, National Herald* and *Sunday Mail* in different capacities.

Sunil Misra, Director (Retd.) Audience Research, All India Radio, New Delhi, is currently working in a senior capacity with the Population Foundation of India.

Horst Mund is currently the Representative of Freidrich Ebert Stiftung in India. An economist from the University of Gottingen, he has been the FES Project Director in West Africa from 1990-92, Desk Officer in the Department of International Development Cooperation of FES from 1992-94 and Incharge of the Project for the Development and Implementation of a Soft-ware Programme from 1994-95. As FES Representative in India, he is actively persuing activities and programmes in communication and media.

Uma Narula, well-known researcher and author of several books, in Consultant, CNET, New Delhi.

Ashok Kumar Panda is the Correspondent of the *Economic Times* at Calcutta. He is the AMIC Zonal Representative (East) in India. He has been Visiting Fellow at the University of Oxford and Past Chairman, PRSI, Orrisa Chapter and Rotary Club of Rourkela. He is on the visiting faculty of several institutes of mass communication in India.

Nandini Prasad is currently working as Programme Officer, Women and Development, in the Netherlands Development Co-operation Section of the Royal Netherlands Embassy in New Delhi. She has been associated with socio-economic issues, of women and children, in both urban and rural areas. For over a decade she has worked in the field of women and development in Bihar and Maharashtra. She has authored two books—'*A Pressing Matter : Women in Press*' and '*A Vision Unveiled : Women in Television*'.

Gopal Saksena, currently Director, Commonwealth Educational Media Centre for Asia (CEMCA), has served All India Radio and Doordarshan in different capacities including Director, Central Production Centre, Controller of Programmes, Director-General Doordarshan; and Director, Satellite Television Centre, Delhi. Also served on the Faculty of Film and TV Institute of India, Pune for about five years from 1975-80. His book, '*Television in India : Changes and Challenges*', brought out by M/S Vikas Publishing House, New Delhi has been well received by press and media circles. He has written over 250 articles on mass media for various national and international journals and newspapers. He was given the Media-India Weston Electronics Award for 1988 for "Outstanding contribution to the electronic media for over three decades."

Radhe Shyam Sharma

Upendra Vajpeyi is the founder General Secretary of the National Media Centre, New Delhi established in 1981. He is a veteran journalist who has worked at several levels in the profession. Among the notable newspapers, he served for more than 10 years are: the daily *Aj* of Varanasi (1950-65) and *Hindustan Times*, New Delhi (1967-82). He was Chairman of the Information Reorganisation Committee set up by the U.P. Govt. in 1975. The report submitted by him became a source material in certain respects for the Second Press Commission set up by the Government of India. He was invited to the UNESCO Conference on Media at Manila in 1983 and the Singapore Conference in 1989. At both the places, he presented the dimensions of the media scene in India as also the regional requirements of media in Asia.

K. Vijayaraghavan is a Senior Scientist, Division of Agricultural Extension, Indian Agricultural Research Institute, New Delhi. He is expert in the areas of Agricultural Development, Administration, Extension Management and Human Resource Development. He has also served as Editor, *Indian Journal of Extension Education* for the last ten years.

INDEX